# ADDICTION

## An Artificially
## Induced Drive

# ADDICTION
## An Artificially Induced Drive

*By*

### NILS BEJEROT, M.D.

*Research Fellow in Drug Dependence*
*Department of Social Medicine*
*Karolinska Institutet*
*Stockholm, Sweden*

*Foreword by*

### S. S. B. Gilder

*Executive Editor, World Medical Journal*

CHARLES C THOMAS • PUBLISHER
*Springfield* • *Illinois* • *U.S.A.*

*Published and Distributed Throughout the World by*
CHARLES C THOMAS • PUBLISHER
BANNERSTONE HOUSE
301-327 East Lawrence Avenue, Springfield, Illinois, U.S.A.

© 1972 by CHARLES C THOMAS • PUBLISHER
ISBN 0-398-02527-4
Library of Congress Catalog Card Number: 72-75906

*With THOMAS BOOKS careful attention is given to all details of manufacturing and design. It is the Publisher's desire to present books that are satisfactory as to their physical qualities and artistic possibilities and appropriate for their particular use. THOMAS BOOKS will be true to those laws of quality that assure a good name and good will.*

*Printed in the United States of America*
X-2

# FOREWORD

When I first introduced my theory on addiction as an artificially induced drive before an international audience in 1970, Dr. S. S. B. Gilder, Executive Editor of the *World Medical Journal,* wrote the following editorial for the *Canadian Medical Association Journal* of which he was a former editor. With the permission of Dr. Gilder and of the *C.M.A.J.* the editorial is reprinted here to serve as a foreword to this book.

HAVE YOU noticed how often in a discussion on drug addiction with various disciplines involved, speakers start by telling the audience that we know little or nothing about the subject; 20 minutes later, they are developing a pet biochemical or psychological or physiological explanation for the phenomenon. Actually, the position is the reverse. We know an enormous amount about the action of drugs, about the psychological make-up of addicts, about the sociology of addiction. What we cannot as yet do is to put our data together and make a sensible explanation of the whole.

Last July in Denmark, Scandinavian psychiatrists heard a paper by a Swedish psychiatrist which attempted to make a synthesis of many pieces of information and produce a unifying theory of addiction. Basically there is perhaps nothing new in his ideas but he puts them together better than most. It is the opinion of Nils Bejerot of the Caroline Institute in Stockholm that addiction is really an artificially induced instinct and that there are two stages in drug dependency. In the first stage the patient is abusing the drug but he is still in control; in the second the process has developed its own dynamics and treatment is now totally different.

Certainly the problem is one that concerns many disciplines, but so often the representatives of these disciplines fail to understand each other and adopt almost a hostile attitude to their colleagues from other specialties. However, all tend to see addiction as a symptom of some chemical, psychologic, social or ethical defect either in the individual or in society. All this seems to Bejerot to be false and sterile. Real addiction, whether to a hard drug or to alcohol, is not a symptom but a deep-seated pathological state with dynamics of its own. Take, for example, tobacco. The adolescent begins to smoke to show his manhood. But 30 years later he is fiercely addicted, though the original need has long since gone. The process has taken over.

This does not support the idea that a person has to have a personality problem or a social problem to become an addict. Any person or any animal can develop a dependency if enough of the substance is introduced into the body for enough time. The greater the addictive properties of the substance, or the more pleasant its pharmacological effects, the quicker and the more effectively will it cause dependency. This latter state must be sharply differentiated from misuse of the drug.

With drug abuse, the patient is still in control; with dependency he has lost control. The period of abuse before dependency begins and the drug takes over varies with the drug. With heroin it is a matter of weeks, with barbiturates it is a matter of months, and with alcohol a matter of years (but the process is accelerated in the young, and so we may see alcoholics in their early twenties). Addiction will set in more quickly if the substance is injected intravenously than if it is taken by mouth. Apes develop alcoholism quite fast with continuous intravenous injection of alcohol.

Bejerot sees an analogy with sex drive. John Doe becomes infatuated with someone and invents all sorts of reasons for absenting himself from the home to be with his new love; soon the affair gets out of control and he is obliged to continue his deceptions whatever the cost. He is hooked, but the tricks he resorts to in order to satisfy his sexual dependency are minor compared with the tricks of the drug addict to get his beloved heroin. In fact we know that addicted men or animals prefer their drug to sex both quantitatively and qualitatively. This gives us some idea of the hardship the drug addict experiences when he is asked to abandon his drug. Would an erring Don Juan consent to castration to cure his ill? The sex deviant usually prefers a life in a closed institution to castration and freedom. As Rado said of drug addiction: "The patient does not suffer from his illness, he enjoys it."

One does not need to be psychiatrically disturbed to prefer pleasure to the sensible way of life; just think of all the enlightened fat people. Or note the common case of the alcoholic who is willing to have his gastritis or other complications treated on condition that he is not deprived of his alcohol.

According to Bejerot, dependency is in fact a short-circuiting of the pain-pleasure principle in which an artificial drive or instinct is created comparable to the sexual instinct or even stronger. This brings us to the results of short-circuiting this defense mechanism. The neurophysiologist Olds has shown us the results of implantation of an electrode into the pleasure centre in the brain of rats. They forget all else but the self-stimulation of the electrode. Seever's experiments with monkeys who were able to inject themselves with narcotics and did so *ad nauseam* are also pertinent. Even in the insect world there are instances of addiction, as is the case of ants which are crazy about a secretion from certain types of beetle. Thus we are dealing with a deep-seated biological phenomenon, of which other examples are seen in the girl with anorexia nervosa, the compulsive gambler or the sex pervert.

The implications of this view of addiction are obvious. Everything possible must be done to prevent the stage of addiction being reached. Once this stage has been reached, appeals to the cooperation of the addict must be strong indeed to break the charmed circle.

S. S. B. GILDER, M.D.

# ACKNOWLEDGMENTS

G UN ZACHARIAS, B.S. in Soc., has for many years been working with the addiction problem. She has read the manuscript of this book and provided many valuable ideas which have been incorporated in the text. My wife Carol Maurice, B.A., S.R.N., has assisted me and translated the book.

NILS BEJEROT

# INTRODUCTION

I
N THE sphere of ideas and science we have constantly to test our theories against the facts and realities we observe. If facts do not fit in with theories, then it is the theories we must scrutinize first. In every field of science we have had to revise our basic theories now and then, for instance the theories that the world is flat and that the sun revolves around the earth. I contend that the facts in addiction, as observed in clinical work, do not fit in with current theories on the nature, spread, and treatment of the condition. In this little book I have principally concentrated on how addiction arises and what it is. I will first describe one of my patients: it is for the reader to decide then if this, and other cases he may himself be acquainted with, are best explained by generally accepted ideas or by the theories I will put forward here.

The case subject was a distinguished, senior physician at a large Swedish hospital, a leading figure in his speciality and active in professional organizations, well-known and respected all over the country. He was open and cheerful, popular with the hospital staff and patients alike. He was a married man in his early fifties with no previous history of abuse of alcohol or drugs. For five years he had been a little worried over periodic impotence, but this had not been problematic enough to cause him to seek psychiatric advice, and his wife had never complained. When on holiday in southern Europe he decided to see if the rumors about the effect of methylphenidate (Ritalin,® Lidepran®) on sexual potency were well-founded. (In Sweden, central stimulants have only been available on special license since 1968, but in many European countries central stimulants are easily available.) In the beginning he took the drug orally. There was no improvement in his impotence, but he continued taking the drugs, and after a few months he went over to intravenous administration. He took the drugs for periods of a few days and nights for up to a week, intersected by periods off drugs. His judgment became so impaired that he worked and attended committee meetings when he was high. His wife consulted prominent psychiatrists, but as the patient was not prepared to undergo voluntary treatment, they considered it impossible to take any action. The addicted physician was frequently psychotic, and then he pulled the furniture to pieces looking for hidden microphones and TV cameras. After some months, his wife could stand no more. She left the wreckage of their luxurious home and rented a room. Her husband became more paranoid when he was alone, and after a few days he joined her. After only a day or two, however, he became severely psychotic; he thought his "enemies" had discovered his whereabouts, and dared not stay any longer. He took a room in a hotel, and within two hours he had pulled the hotel room to pieces searching for microphones and TV cameras. The police were called, and as consultant psychiatrist to the police I was asked to examine him at the police station. He recognized me at once, and asked for protection against an international TV gang that was filming him day and night from the ceiling, and were operating now in the room where we were sitting. He also wanted me to explain to the police "and other idiots who think I am insane" that he was in his right mind. The period between taking the first tablet of Ritalin and his arrest and admission to a mental hospital was just one year.

Current ideas that addiction is a symptom of social or psychological maladjustment, alienation, disillusionment and distress over national and international developments, bad homes or parents and so on, hardly apply here. This intelligent, pleasant and successful man was in a very privileged economic position. His relations with his wife were good, and he was one of the least alienated men I know. Whether or not he had loving parents I cannot say, but they had anyway not prevented him from advancing to the top of his profession or from enjoying a full and apparently satisfying private life. The detail that caused him to try central stimulants, his intermittent impotence, is extremely common in men of his age, a fact that is well-known to every physician.

My theory of addiction, briefly, is that the condition is caused by dependence upon drugs, and an effect of the drug itself, completely independent of the factor causing the individual to commence his abuse. Often the initial abuse is completely incidental: curiosity, the desire to belong to an in-group or careless medical treatment. The incident that started the individual off on drugs has, however, nothing to do with the course of the condition once addiction is established. In my opinion, addiction develops the strength and character of basic drives, and it is as difficult for an addict to break his addiction as for ordinary people to suppress their sexual drives. This theory, and theories on the spread of drug epidemics, their relation to drug policy, and on ways of combatting these epidemics, are described in the text.

N. B.

# CONTENTS

# ADDICTION

An Artificially
Induced Drive

# Chapter 1

# WHAT IS ADDICTION?

ADDICTION may be described as "the compulsive use of chemical agents which are harmful to the individual, to society, or to both" (Wikler 1953). These chemicals affect the nervous system in a pleasurable way. The individual quickly learns to appreciate the effects, and after a while it is very difficult or almost impossible to give up the drug. The drug dependence has then gained the strength and character of a basic drive—the craving or hunger for the drug has developed into a need which may be as strong or even stronger than sexual desire. The use or abuse of drugs has developed into a severe illness, addiction, and the drug abuser has become a drug addict.

Most forms of addiction have a pleasant introductory phase, sometimes called the "honeymoon" period, but sooner or later the negative effects and difficulties arise, often with terrific force.

The addict seldom realizes that he is gradually becoming dependent before it is too late and the addiction has mastered him. Even if he now really wants to stop, it is rare, at this stage, that an addict is able to resist his craving for the drug. Those who have tried to overcome a mild type of drug dependence, like smoking, may have some idea of the impelling forces slumbering far beneath the conscious level of our volitional life.

In popular debate, we often hear that addiction is only a *symptom* of maladjustment, psychological disturbances, or social grievances. In Sweden, advocates of this theory have even gone so far as to proclaim that nothing of permanent value can be done about this symptom until the underlying social or psychological causes have been dealt with. Those who are working with the addiction problem have been told that they should go out and change the character of our civilization and that then

3

the drug question will solve itself, both as an individual and a social problem.

## ADDICTION: A CONDITION OF ITS OWN

I contend that the above line of reasoning is based on a misconception. While *drug abuse* is often a symptom of mal-adjustment, this is by no means always the case, and when *addiction* supervenes it is never a symptom but a morbid condition in itself with its own character and dynamics. Let me illustrate this argument in relation to tobacco smoking, which is one of the most banal of all drug dependences, in spite of the fact that it causes a considerable amount of sickness and a clearly increased death rate. Most people who smoke started in the lower teens (or even earlier), usually to imitate their elders and to look grown-up. In the beginning it was often unpleasant and the youngsters suffered from headache and vomiting, but they coughed their way through one packet of cigarettes after the other to prove to themselves and others how grown-up they were.

If the ambition to look big was the *underlying cause* which induced the teenager to *begin* smoking, this can hardly explain why the same person, 30 years later, may be smoking a pack of cigrettes a day. The "cause"—to look grown-up—no longer exists, but the individual, as we know, nonetheless finds it very difficult to stop smoking. Why? I say it is because he has developed a nicotine dependence. Cigarette smoking is now no longer a symptom. The craving for cigarettes has become *a condition of its own*, a "disease" if you like, and far more serious than some of our commonest illnesses, such as dandruff, warts, and caries.

From this example of cigarette smoking we can immediately conclude that *no disturbed personality and no underlying social problems are required for an individual to develop a drug dependence. In principle, any individual and any animal will develop an addiction of this type if certain substances are administered in certain quantities during a certain period of time.* The more potent a dependence-producing substance, the quicker is the development of addiction. I am prepared to say that all my readers, after only a few weeks of continual use of cocaine, would long for the drug for the rest of their lives; so strong and pleasurable are the effects of cocaine in the early stage of abuse.

The established drug dependence thus becomes a force in itself and follows its own laws. We could agree with the 19th century German philosopher Hegel, and say that in these processes a dialectic change occurs in the development: A certain quality ("abuse" or experimental, precompulsive smoking), after successive quantitative increments (that is repeated experimental smoking), changes to a completely *new quality* ("dependence," and in this case "nicotinism").

Drug dependence is thus, in principle, a condition essentially different from drug abuse. Even if there are intermediary stages that are difficult to classify, in most cases it should not cause the trained clinician any great difficulty to differentiate abusers from those who have passed the precompulsive phase and developed a well-established addiction.

## THE PLEASURE-PAIN PRINCIPLE

It seems as if the pleasure-pain principle is the primary biological steering mechanism for the whole animal world, including humans. To obtain a reward—whether it is to eat and drink, to find warmth, security, and friendship or to obtain sexual satisfaction—some kind of effort is required. In the same way effort is needed in order to avoid discomfort—irrespective of whether it is hunger, thirst, pain, cold, loneliness, sexual deprivation etc. *We can say that the pleasure-pain principle is the unconscious regulator in the animal world and it furthers the adjustment of the individual and the survival of the species. I look upon euphoric or pleasurable drug effects as a kind of short-circuiting of this pleasure-pain principle, and the final result as an artificially induced drive with the strength and character of a basic drive, which may be even stronger than sexual craving.*

The artificially induced drives, contrary to the natural drives, tend to bring about a deterioration in individual adaptation and social functioning. It is probably an intuitive understanding of this situation that has led to the old moral, political, and religious attitudes requiring that pleasure shall be "earned," "deserved."

Addiction has a strong tendency to lead towards social insufficiency, and it is the other members of society who have to shoulder the responsibilities of those who fall out. Socially the result is that the addict becomes pacified in an egocentric pleasure-consumption at the expense of the working population.

When a drug addiction has been established, the individual loses control over his drug consumption and his craving dominates the addict and his way of life. In the sphere of the drug craving, the individual's normal free will is put out of action. In one sense it is true that, as the addict often says, "I could stop tomorrow if I really wanted to," but they don't want to, just because the drug craving steers their volitional life. The addict, however, retains some power of modifying his behavior. For a long while he may manage to conceal his drug consumption or direct it into socially accepted forms. The alcoholic, a person addicted to alcohol, may remain sober at work and perhaps even when driving. The same applies also to the average person in regard to basic drives—he can wait until mealtime when he is hungry, and refrain from accosting attractive women he does not know. Even though the individual has considerable freedom in forming the details around the desired experience, he has enormous difficulty in suppressing his natural drives.

The Canadian neurophysiologist Olds (1954) demonstrated on laboratory rats the course of behavior when animals are given the opportunity of directly stimulating the pleasure center in the brain. Olds placed small platinum electrodes into the rat brain and connected these with a switch in the cage. When the animals touched the switch they connected a weak electric current and evidently obtained a very pleasurable sensation. The rats then "succumbed to the vice" of treading on the switch thousands of times a day, and continued to stimulate themselves until they fell down exhausted or dead.

The strength of the addict's desire for drugs compared to sexual drives can easily be tested. I often ask my addicted patients in prison what they would choose if they were offered the alternative of as much alcohol as they wanted for one evening or a plentiful supply of drugs. They all laugh and say at once that they would choose the drugs. Then I ask these young men, who have been without women for a long time, whether they would choose a night with an attractive sexual partner or a night with a supply of drugs. Very few hesitate, but most of them reply at once that they would prefer the drugs.

When the intensity of the craving for drugs exceeds sexual craving it shows what a tremendous force is operating in drug dependence, and we should not be astonished at the poor results of treatment.

It is instructive in this connection to study the alcoholic. It is not unusual for him to drink away his money, family, job, social position, self-respect, and everything that previously was important to him. The only explanation of how he can accept this slow, psychological, economic, and social deterioration is that the successive painful losses are outweighed by the satisfaction that alcohol gives him, otherwise he would stop drinking.

Willpower and desires often collide in everyday life, and we need not be psychologically disturbed or weak-willed individuals to be unable to master our desires. We need only think of all the fat people who so whole-heartedly desire to be thin. The desire to eat tempting food, however, is usually stronger, and for that reason their curves increase with the years. Consider then that the craving for drugs in most kinds of addiction is much more insistent than the desire for cream cakes.

Obese patients provide many parallels with addicts. They are often quite incapable of steering developments in spite of strong medical support; they are unreliable in reporting what they consume; they often insist that they "just haven't taken anything at all" although they continue to gain weight. If they are admitted to a hospital for weight reduction (weaning) they have a great tendency to smuggle in unpermitted calories, and after discharge there is a very high risk of relapse into over-eating and obesity.

Gambling is another condition which appears to have some relationship to addiction in so far as it seems to have the irrational element of a basic drive. A game that for most people seems quite meaningless and in the long run leads to loss for the player is experienced by the inveterate gambler as so pleasurable that he can discontinue only with difficulty, if he can stop at all. Although the player knows that he has the odds against him and that the man manipulating the roulette, totalizator, Bingo or lottery earns large sums out of his activity, the gambler does not stop playing until his money is gone or the premises are closed (Moran 1970). Just as in drug addiction, gambling is often accompanied by cultural and social declination. Ruin and suicide are often the final stage in both conditions.

If addiction is regarded as behavior of an instinctive type, it is easier to understand the characteristic behavior which develops in addiction. Generations of physicians have deplored the addict's deception and unreliability. This is usually misunderstood and regarded as a proof of deeply rooted character disorders existing prior to the development of addiction. The phenomenon, however, is a natural defense mechanism in protecting basic drives. We know that individuals who are usually very honest and reliable lie when they have to protect an extramarital love affair which is vital to them. Folklore reflects this situation in the saying "all is fair in love and war."

Rado (1963) captured something of the most essential element in addiction when he said: "The patient does not suffer from his illness, he enjoys it." Naturally the addict suffers from all the complications of his dependence, and he will seek help for these physical, psychological, and social side effects; but even when he fully understands what lies at the root of his problem he is seldom prepared to give up his special form of enjoyment. Heavy smokers can spend much time and money consulting specialists for a chronic bronchitis, and they are willing to try the most distasteful cough mixtures, but they are usually not prepared to accept the only adequate measure—to stop smoking. The same applies to alcoholics. If they really want to stop drinking they can take disulfiram (Antabuse®), but they are rarely prepared to accept this treatment.

## ADDICTION IN THE ANIMAL WORLD

Drug addiction is by no means confined to humans. It also occurs in nature especially among some social insects, particularly ants and termites—a situation which can hardly be explained away by the psychological and social "symptom" theory.

Among insects that may develop a drug dependence is a common Scandinavian ant, *Lasius flavus*, which harbors and feeds small beetles, *Claviger* and *Lomechusa*. When the ants have given their beetle guests food they hurry to obtain a secretion from a tuft of hairs on the beetle's body. This secretion is obviously greatly desired by the ants, but it is of no nutritional

The yellow ant, *Lasius flavus*, seeking her "drug"—the secretion from the *Claviger* beetle. Photo by Lennart Nilsson, Sweden.

value. When they are disturbed, the ants carry the beetles to safety before they save their own offspring. Hölldobler (1971), in a fascinating study of ants and rove beetles, showed that the presence of beetle larvae in an ant community reduced the normal flow of food to ant larvae, but that the presence of ant larvae did not affect the flow of food to beetle larvae. Beetle larvae also feed on the ants' own eggs and larvae, but are nonetheless tolerated and protected in the ant community. These phenomena lead one's thoughts to the opium smokers of ancient China who, it is said, even sold their wives and children to obtain opium.

Seevers (1969) has reported that in various countries horses and cattle that discover locoweeds and come under their influence refuse other fodder, greedily seek them, and even influence other animals to eat them, often with fatal results.

### Addiction in Monkeys

Seevers has also carried out one of the most interesting series of animal experiments in the field of addiction research. With the help of some elaborate apparatus he arranged that a number of rhesus monkeys were themselves able to administer various addicting drugs intravenously. A narrow tube was inserted through the monkey's back and connected to a blood vessel. The monkey was provided with a harness and the tubes were led through flexible arms from the harness to an injection apparatus outside the cage. The monkey could move freely in its cage, and was apparently quite unaffected by the apparatus attached to it. Inside the cage there was a bar which the monkey had to find itself. When the monkey pressed the bar—first out of playfulness or curiosity—it immediately received an intravenous dose of the drug being tested.

Figure 1. Stills from a film by Maurice H. Seevers, Ann Arbor. a) A monkey dependent upon morphine through prolonged self-administration: Here enjoying the effects of the drug. b) A monkey repeating his dose by pressing a bar. c) A monkey dependent upon barbiturates through prolonged self-administration: Here suffering from abstinence convulsions.

The monkeys quickly developed a severe dependence and became very ill. In spite of this they continued to take more and

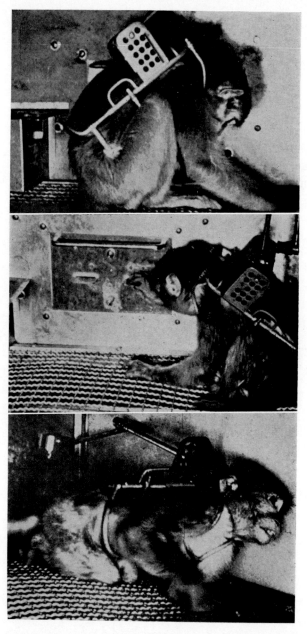

more of the drugs and were quite unable to reduce their drug consumption or refrain altogether. The experiment with central stimulants (amphetamine) was particularly interesting. The monkeys took the drug according to exactly the same injection pattern as severely addicted amphetaminists. The monkeys injected repeatedly day and night for five to seven days without sleep and with very little food or drink. At the end of this period they were exhausted and slept for a few days. After that they ate and drank and then started again on the next intensive injection period of about a week, and so on.

This pattern of abuse with periods of about a week of intensive injections intersected by a few days' rest is purely pharmacologically conditioned. It is caused by exhaustion and dehydration resulting from the intensive administration of central stimulants, and the depletion of transmittor substances in the brain.

Seevers then took his monkeys out of the cages, let them rest a few weeks and regain full physical health. After that he replaced them in their cages, put on the harness and connected the tubes; but this time he did not open the taps to the injection apparatus.

The result was extremely interesting. It was found that the monkeys who had developed a dependence upon heroin pressed the bar about 2,000 times before they gave up. The monkeys dependent on amphetamine pressed the bar even more often. In this way Seevers has shown the strength of psychological dependence on drugs which is the nucleus in addiction, and causes the frequent relapses after treatment. The physical abstinence symptoms which were previously the main focus of interest are not today any great medical problem when treated properly in hospitals. After one or two weeks all physical abstinence symptoms have disappeared. In fact, tolerance and physical abstinence have nothing to do with addiction, but represent temporary metabolic complications after high consumption of depressive drugs (opiates, barbiturates, alcohol, solvents etc.), and these phenomena do not occur—or are negligible—after consumption of stimulant drugs (cocaine, amphetamine and other synthetic stimulants; LSD, mescaline, cannabis and other hallucinogens). It is the *psychological dependence*, the prolonged craving for repeated drug experiences, and the abrupt return of the pattern of advanced consumption, which constitutes addiction. Animals and humans react in very much the same way to the various drugs.

These are physiological and pharmacological phenomena that must be understood and borne in mind. At the beginning of this century, however, these facts were not generally accepted. The great pharmacologist, Louis Lewin (1964), says in his famous book *Phantastica*: "I have seen among men of science frightful symptoms due to the craving for cocaine. Those who believe they can enter the temple of happiness through this gate of pleasure purchase their momentary delights at the cost of body and soul."

In practice, as we know, the great majority of people avoid exposing themselves to the risk of becoming addicted quite simply by not experimenting with these dangerous drugs. *The use of addicting preparations is medically defensible only in definite morbid conditions, and then, of course, under strict and competent medical control. All other use of these drugs is to be regarded as abuse.*

## Chapter 2

# WHAT ARE NARCOTICS?

THE WORD narcotics comes originally from the Greek word *nárke* which means sleep. It was opium abuse, the main form of addiction in ancient times, which formed the terminology. Opium produces lassitude and sleepiness, and opium smoking usually terminates with a few hours deep sleep. The term narcotics has, however, come to include other severely addicting drugs, for instance cocaine, which do not lead to drowsiness or sleep, but to the exact opposite.

## A LEGAL TERM

*"Narcotics" is now purely a legal term:* It simply refers to the drugs which are included in The Single Convention of 1961: opium, morphine, certain morphine derivatives and substitutes for these, and also coca leaves, cocaine, and cannabis preparations such as hashish and marijuana. These substances are thus classed as narcotic drugs practically all over the world. East and West are in complete agreement about the necessity of a restrictive drug policy, and few international agreements have met with such massive support as have the international narcotic agreements.

Apart from the substances which are internationally classified as narcotic drugs, every country has the right to class as narcotics within their own boundaries other addicting drugs which have given rise to, or threaten to give rise to severe abuse. In Scandinavia, a number of synthetic central stimulants (amphetamine and fenmetrazin, better known by the trade name Preludin®, and several others) have been classed as narcotics. The same applies to LSD and certain other hallucinogens (mescaline, psilocybin etc.).

LSD has been classed as a narcotic drug in many countries,

but has not yet been included in the international conventions. The central stimulants and the raw materials from which they are produced were, until 1969, classed as narcotics in only a few countries because they have hitherto been subject to advanced abuse in a limited number of places. The severe form of addiction they give rise to has not previously been widely recognized internationally.

In January 1969, however, the UN Commission on Narcotic Drugs, on Swedish initiative, recommended all countries to introduce strict control over central stimulants also. At a UN conference in Vienna in January 1971 a further important step was taken towards including central stimulants in the international narcotic convention.

## A MEDICAL TERM

In 1964 the World Health Organization (WHO) adopted a new terminology in the field of addiction. Severe forms of disease had previously been called *drug addiction* and mild forms *drug habituation.* WHO now merged its previous concepts into a single term: *drug dependence.*

I would prefer "toxicomania" as a scientific term for all the various kinds and degrees of dependence, regardless of whether the poisons are classed as narcotics, ordinary drugs or simply alcohol, thinner, trichloroethylene or other substances (Bejerot 1970).

## ADDICTING SUBSTANCES ORIGINS AND EFFECTS

There is a number of very dissimilar substances, natural products, and synthetic preparations which may give rise to addiction. I will go systematically through the most important substances, their origin, and effects. First, a few words on the effects of dependence-producing drugs in general.

Comparative forms of the two adjectives, "dangerous" and "strong," occur often in the debate concerning drugs. I have already mentioned that nicotinism is a banal drug dependence. Naturally this does not mean that nicotine is a weak or safe drug. If anyone should eat a Havana cigar or inject the corresponding amount of nicotine solution into his veins, he would hardly have an opportunity of witnessing on how strong a poison nicotine is.

To obtain an objective estimate of the effect of an active substance compared to another variant of the same substance, it is necessary to administer the same dose of the active substances, and in the same way. For instance, the intoxicating effect of 20 centiliters (cl) whiskey is naturally greater than that of 20 cl beer. A pipeful of hashish is a more effective intoxicant than a similar pipeful of marijuana, although both the first cases concerned alcohol and both the second cannabis.

The effect of the active substance measured in this way has misled many people into concluding that whiskey must be more dangerous than beer and hashish than marijuana. It is clear, however, that the current Swedish policy of steering alcohol consumption towards weaker variations (beer and wine instead of spirits) has not led to a reduction of the damage caused by alcohol, but rather to an increase in alcoholism among the youth (beer alcoholism). The idea that beer is "not dangerous" combined with its availability has led to a consumption of beer in certain youth circles on a scale which we previously only saw among elderly, chronic alcoholics.

Thus if we compare two drugs A and B, and say that the effect of drug A is greater than that of drug B, we mean that it takes more of drug B than of drug A to obtain the same effect, but that both drugs can produce the same effect. An individual smokes, let us say, five pipefuls of marijuana in succession and obtains the same effect as if he smoked one pipeful of hashish; or we drink two or three beers instead of a whiskey and reach a similar degree of intoxication.

Another way of comparing the strength of one drug with another is the following: Drug A is stronger than drug B. By that we mean that the effect of drug A is qualitatively greater than the effect of drug B, practically regardless of the size of the dose. As an example we can take morphine and aspirin.

## Opiates

Opium has been known for thousands of years, and was described by Homer in the *Odyssey*. Raw opium is obtained from the opium poppy which is cultivated in a warm, dry belt from the Balkans, over Asia Minor, the Middle East, Afghanistan, India, Thailand, Burma, and South China.

The greatest opium producing country today is Thailand, where the mountain tribes (about 200,000 individuals) in the inaccessible areas bordering upon Burma and Laos have for centuries had opium cultivation as their most important source of income. They live in such a remote area that it is said there are no other products worth transporting to the outer world (UN Survey 1967). With a little goodwill this problem could be overcome, however. The real problem is the enormous profit earned by the many links in the chain of distribution.

WHO reckons that only about one-tenth of the world opium production is used for medical purposes, the rest is diverted to various forms of abuse. The eastern smuggle route is over the Philippines and Hong Kong to USA; the western route over the Middle East to Italy and the south of France, where the opium and morphine are usually turned into heroin which is four to five times as potent as morphine.

### Opiate Addiction

The effects of morphine are so strong that they completely dominate the effects of raw opium. Heroin has a shorter effect than morphine, only two or three hours compared to four to five hours for morphine.

There are a number of morphine substitutes (methadone, dextromoramide, etc.) which have been synthesized in the hope of avoiding addiction risks. Even if research in this field in recent years has led to promising results, e.g. pentazocin (Talwin®), there are still many dangerous substitutes used in medical practice.

Medically, opiates are principally used for their strong analgesic effects. They also give a sensation of calm and well-being, which is of benefit for operation and accident patients.

It is characteristic for all preparations in the opiate group that the dose must usually be slowly increased to maintain or repeat the effects. This is called *tolerance* development.

In extreme cases, morphinists-heroinists can reach 50 times

the lethal dose for ordinary people, and a couple of hundred times the usual medical dose.

When the drug leaves the body, severe physical abstinence symptoms occur (rise in temperature, muscular pain, nausea, persistant vomiting, diarrhea, etc.) which make the patient try to obtain the drug at practically any price.

The heightened mood and the sensation of well-being or "bliss" (euphoria) will lead to dependence even in persons who are not in pain. Just a few weeks of abuse—or careless medical treatment —can suffice to initiate a severe addiction.

Dependence develops particularly rapidly on intravenous injection of morphine and heroin. Here the first injection may give such an intensely pleasurable sensation ("kick") that a psychological dependence can develop even before physical dependence arises.

The pleasurable effects, however, soon fall into the background. After an intense honeymoon with morphine or heroin, the addict usually has to fight a continual battle to retain the original effect and sensations, and ultimately to limit the unpleasantness and depression and to regain an ordinary, normal mental condition. This has been called the struggle for "negative euphoria." Relief of pain is experienced as pleasurable, even if the pain does not disappear completely; in a condition of distress the individual strives to reduce this distress, and if he succeeds this is experienced as pleasurable.

After weaning from the drug, the euphoric or pleasurable effects increase again when the drug contact is renewed, and the individual may then for a short time manage with low doses until tolerance develops and requires increased doses. Many opiate addicts wander round and round in this circle of abuse, weaning, renewed abuse and so on.

All opiates reduce sexual drive. Male morphinists often become impotent, while menstruation may discontinue in female opiate addicts. They themselves often interpret the cessation of menstruation as pregnancy.

### Cocaine and Synthetic Central Stimulants

Cocaine comes from the coca bush which flourishes in the warm, subtropical valleys of the Andes. When the Spanish con-

querors landed in South America in 1533 they came into contact
with coca chewing Indians. Coca leaves contain about 1 to 2
percent cocaine and when they are chewed, very small quantities
of cocaine are released. Such a chewing dose has a very short
effect, about 40 minutes, and this—*a cocada*—was not only the
old measurement of time in the Andes, but also was the measurement of distance. A man could walk under the influence of a
mouthful of coca leaves about three kilometers on level land and
two kilometers in the mountains.

The purified cocaine is a very strong central stimulant, but
*the effects are essentially the same as those produced by syn-
thetic central stimulants which are abused on a large scale in
Sweden—amphetamine, Preludin and Ritalin.* The difference
lies in the strength of the drug, but the addicts compensate for
this by taking larger doses of the synthetic preparations.

### Rapid Development of Dependence

Cocaine quickly gives rise to addiction and the dependence is
extremely intensive and resistant to treatment. No unpleasant
physical abstinence symptoms arise when the effects of cocaine
disappear. Even *the synthetic central stimulants do not give rise
to physical abstinence symptoms in the usual sense of the term.*

Fatigue, hunger, and thirst are eliminated under the influence
of all central stimulants, mood is raised, self-confidence increases
—sometimes to the point of "delusions of grandeur"—inhibitions
are relaxed, and judgment blunted.

There is restless, disordered activity, and it has long been
pointed out in the scientific literature that central stimulants
give rise to criminal activity. These effects spring from the
tendency of abusers to overrate themselves and underestimate
difficulties and the consequences of their actions.

As with opiates, the toxic effects soon become more important
to the addict than anything else. In the intensive form of abuse
that dominates in Sweden (repeated intravenous injections of
large doses three to ten times a day for perhaps a week at a
time, with a few days rest between drug periods) the patient's
condition deteriorates rapidly in every way—medically, socially,
intellectually, and morally.

### Dangerous "Manias" and Personality Changes

Both cocaine and synthetic central stimulants have a tendency to cause acute conditions reminiscent of schizophrenia, among addicts called "noia" (from paranoia). The patient becomes suspicious, hears voices, feels he is being persecuted, develops great anxiety, and acts in a peculiar way, sometimes in panic.

Many of my patients have provided examples of very peculiar "noias." One took down the wallpaper in his room and washed it in the bath "to find small microphones which have been mounted into the wallpaper." Another picked his suit to pieces at the seams: He explained that there were "crystals in the seams and these threads are part of the secret crystal receiving sets."

It is very common for "noia" to take violent forms, often endangering both the patient's life and that of others. One of my patients threw himself out of a window on the second or third floor because he had hallucinations and thought he heard his fiancée (who did not even know where he was!) threatening to break down the door with an axe and kill him. Since he had stood in the window a long while calling for help, he landed in a fireman's net.

Another paranoic addict threw out most of the furniture from his flat several flights up. He had an idea that the building was surrounded by plainclothed police and he tried to hit them with the furniture, which he aimed at pedestrians in the street.

These patients must, of course, be taken under care immediately and admitted to a mental hospital. The acute psychosis usually passes after a few days or a week, but lasting personality changes have been reported. Some amphetaminists have become more suspicious after prolonged addiction to central stimulants, and chronic amphetamine psychoses occur even if they are rare. They are very reminiscent of schizophrenia, but usually they can be differentiated from this condition.

### Pharmacological Basis of Gang Abuse

The central stimulants work in a remarkable way which explains why these drugs are taken in gangs, while the morphinist and heroinist, for instance, usually takes his injections alone or together with a few friends.

As early as 1942 Chance, during experiments on rats, discovered that the effect of a certain dose of amphetamine was augmented in direct proportion to the number of rats (up to ten) that he had placed in the same cage! If he put ten rats in the cage instead of one, he needed only to give one tenth of the amount to reach the same effect.

Our ordinary gang abuse in the "dens" seems to be a psychological and sociological phenomenon which is essentially pharmacologically conditioned.

Quite unconsciously, the addicts "economize" with their drugs by collecting in dens and by drawing new abusers into the circle. This mechanism then contributes to the very rapid spread of this type of addiction.

We have long known that cocainism is one of the addictions which is most difficult to cure. It was not previously realized, however, that the synthetic central stimulants (amphetamine, Preludin, Ritalin) give rise to practically the same symptoms as cocaine.

## Hallucinogens

There are a number of natural products and synthetic preparations which bring about changes in our sensations and also can produce hallucinations. Hashish and marijuana come from the Indian hemp, *Cannabis sativa,* which is a tall and hardy grass that grows in subtropical, dry climates. The pharmacological effects of the plant were known in prehistoric times. From the top shoots and flowers of the female plant *marijuana* is prepared; it looks like something between finely cut tobacco and chopped string.

*Hashish* is the resin from the female flowers. It is dried and then turns dark brown or almost black and becomes very hard. It is usually smuggled in the form of large cakes and is sold in small pieces which look like crumbled India rubber. Hashish has a faint smell, but when it is lighted it smoulders and gives off strong smoke smelling like sweet, oriental incense.

Hashish is cut into small pieces and almost always smoked in a pipe. Marijuana, which is bulkier and far weaker, is often smoked in hand-rolled cigarettes called "reefers."

### Short-term Effects

Hashish smoking causes an intoxication which is somewhat like that of alcohol: heightened mood, increased self-confidence, deterioration in judgment, lowered inhibitory functions.

Under the influence of hashish there is marked flight of ideas, and the individuals become giggly. Quite unmotivated laughter occurs.

Sensations of sight and hearing alter during hashish intoxication. The abuser has difficulty in judging time and distance; he even has difficulty in judging the length of his own limbs. This, together with the fact that muscle coordination deteriorates, sometimes results in serious misjudgments. Hashish smokers are therefore dangerous on the roads, both as drivers and pedestrians.

On greater intoxication, visual illusions and pseudo-hallucinations occur when the eyes are closed. In this stage there is a dissolution of the ego: Reality glides away and the hashish smoker feels that he experiences "a unity with the Universe" or he "sees the inner meaning of things."

After a few hours the intoxication passes over. The hashish smoker then realizes quite clearly that the peculiar sensations were effects of intoxication.

If a hashish smoker is disturbed during intoxication he easily becomes irritable. In addition, severe agitation sometimes occurs (a bad trip) during strong hashish intoxication: The individual experiences frightening hallucinations and grotesque delusions about what is happening around him, and may then act in panic.

Flashbacks or echo effects, so common in abuse of strong hallucinogens such as LSD, occasionally occur also in cannabis abuse, and the addicts call them "clean trips." New drug effects may then be experienced weeks or even months after the last dose.

### Long-term Effects

Even if the intoxication passes over quickly, from prolonged hashish smoking a changed interpretation of reality often develops. Our ordinary reality is experienced by the heavy hashish smoker as increasingly uninteresting and meaningless, while the intoxication experiences become more important and essential. The heavy hashish smoker tends to lose interest in school or work, he becomes passive and is very inclined to glide into a life of daydreams.

The altered interpretation of reality does not only affect his experience of today and tomorrow, but of the past also. Time and time again we see hashish smokers who, during their childhood, were active and happy and afterwards remember this period as a nightmare.

It is now known that the active substance in cannabis is stored in certain brain cells, and this may be an important explanation of the chronic effects of cannabis smoking.

## Hashish Psychoses

Severe insanity (psychosis) initiated by hashish smoking is a familiar phenomenon in the Arab countries. In Sweden we are now beginning to see an increase in the number of hashish psychoses also.

These conditions are more serious than the amphetamine psychoses. They last far longer, often for months, and in some cases become chronic.

I have seen several young people who, following a single hashish psychosis, have suffered from very serious personality changes which will probably be permanent and lead to life-long incapacity.

The active component in cannabis, tetrahydrocannabinol (THC), can now be synthesized. When given experimentally in extremely small doses, it causes an immediate psychotic condition. When given experimentally to rhesus monkeys, THC alters their behavior. Normally they are active and aggressive, but when given THC they sit still with a contemplative expression on their faces. The attendant can put his finger in a monkey's mouth without this eliciting any reaction (Edery 1970).

There is a marked increase in the number of reports now appearing in the scientific press on the deleterious effects of cannabis. For instance a British team demonstrated, by means of roentgen examinations, atrophy of brain tissue in heavy cannabis smokers (Campbell *et al.* 1971).

### The Hippie World

Early in 1968 I saw a shocking example of how hashish smoking can change people's attitude and way of life.

During a journey to study addiction in the Far East, I stopped for a few days in New Delhi. The Indian authorities told me that the first hippies had come to New Delhi in 1966. At the time of my visit (January 1968) more than 500 hippies had been registered during the previous six months in one of the four districts of the city. The Indians were very confused over this peculiar invasion.

I spent most of my stay in New Delhi among these hippies. Almost all of those I came into contact with were former European or American university students, and they had all smoked hashish for a long time. I spoke to dozens of them, and they were all agreed that they definitely had finished with modern industrial society. Most of them intended to continue to travel up to Nepal and the Himalayan slopes and live there. Many said they aimed at becoming Buddhist monks.

These hippies were long haired and bearded. They wore unusual clothes and some had hung bells around their necks. A few of them had the *Medieval Tibetian Book of Death* in their pocket and treated it as a holy writ. They got along on their savings or money their relatives sent, on the hospitality of the Indians or, according to the police, to some extent also on illicit trade in drugs.

It is difficult to say how much of this is a new fad and how much is due to the long-term effects of hashish. The more I have seen of hashish veterans the more convinced I have become that hashish, in time, leads people away from an ordered form of life. The attitude to life of veteran hashish smokers in many ways is so reminiscent of some Oriental societies with their passivity, unworldliness, tendency to mysticism and fatalism —that one wonders to what degree these old and largely stagnant cultures are marked by the effects of the drug. On the other hand, the Asiatic countries which have resisted dangerous drugs, or overcome their drug problem—Israel, Japan and China—all present a dynamic development.

Karl Evang, WHO expert and head of the Norwegian Board of Health, a well-known left wing politician, has declared that if hashish became as widely used as alcohol, all ordered social life, as we know it, would cease to function within a decade or two.

LSD was synthesized as early as 1938, but it lay unused in a Swiss laboratory until 1943, when its remarkable effects were discovered by chance. Dr. Albert Hofmann, who had produced it, happened to imbibe microscopic amounts of the drug and experienced the first LSD psychosis.

The effects of LSD are, in principle, of the same nature as those of hashish, but far stronger and more profound. A 50-millionth part of a gram is enough to produce a psychosis of schizophrenic character which lasts six to ten hours.

Weeks and months after a single dose, new psychotic attacks may occur quite spontaneously. I have had patients who have suffered from prolonged mental illness after a single LSD dose. Some of them will probably never be well again.

From what has been said, one may easily get the impression that cannabis is "milder" and LSD "stronger." Probably the situation is rather that very few cannabis smokers consume cannabis preparations in such quantities that the effect of the intoxication reaches that of an LSD intoxication. The long-term effects, however, may be the same. In addition, as I have already said, the active substance in Indian hemp can now be synthesized, and it has proven to be very strong indeed, with an intoxicating effect comparable to that of LSD.

In the United States a cult, revolving around LSD was started by Timothy Leary and Richard Alpert, associate professors in psychology at Harvard University. When chromosome changes were reported in LSD abusers and their children the cult involving this preparation waned somewhat. Several signs suggest that in the U. S. there is a fall in the popularity of the hippie movement with its romantic and anarchistic character.

## Tranquilizers, Sleeping Drugs and Alcohol

Certain tranquilizers and sleeping drugs can give rise to severe dependence if the dosage instructions are exceeded.

Among sleeping drugs it is particularly the barbiturates which may give rise to severe addiction with a risk of epileptic attacks and extreme confusion during the abstinence period. Often this development of abuse arises through a gradual increase by the patient of medicine prescribed in ordinary doses. The individual becomes more and more dependent on the drug.

It is well-known that alcohol can also cause very serious dependence. Chronic alcoholism is, in principle, an addiction. Alcohol hunger is for the alcoholic compelling and inexorable. When alcohol leaves the body, alcoholics may suffer from severe physical abstinence symptoms such as trembling, sweating, palpitations etc. In severe cases, delirium tremens develops. This is a dangerous psychotic condition which untreated frequently leads to death through acute circulatory collapse.

## Thinner Sniffing

Many substances in addition to those mentioned may be abused with a view toward intoxication, and then also give rise to severe dependence. We can mention thinner, the very toxic solvent trichloroethylene, and also benzene glues etc.

It is the tolulene component in thinner which is mainly responsible for the intoxicating effects through its high volatility and power to dissolve fats (brain substance consists mainly of special fatty tissue).

Thinner sniffing is definitely an abuse of young people. The sniffer saturates a rag with the solvent and holds it in front of his nose and mouth, breathing in deeply. After about 10 to 15 inspirations, an intoxication develops which in all essentials— except for the smell—resembles alcohol inebriation. The intoxication passes over quickly if it is not kept up with further sniffing. Often the sniffing is practiced continuously for several hours; 24-hour sniffing has even been reported.

A certain amount of tolerance develops on intensive sniffing, that is, the individual tolerates and requires larger doses. The symptoms of abuse which arise after a time are the same as in alcoholism: irritability, sometimes agitation, outbreaks of rage, sleeplessness etc. In advanced abuse there may be severe abstinence symptoms in the form of sweating, trembling, and even delirium tremens.

Damage to the liver and bone marrow may occur. Trichloroethylene is particularly poisonous, and sniffing this substance has in many cases led to death through acute respiratory depression.

Experience shows that sniffing occurs principally among idle teenagers. Around a little nucleus of a few maladjusted youths, large epidemics may quickly flame up. This gang phenomena usually ceases if the nucleus group is taken in hand by the Child Welfare authorities for treatment. Intractable thinner sniffers generally go over to abuse of alcohol or hard drugs in the upper teens.

It is also worth noting that *multiple addiction,* that is, the simultaneous, advanced abuse of several quite different substances (e.g. alternatively stimulating and tranquilizing drugs, hashish, alcohol etc.) is becoming more common in industrialized countries.

Differences between various nerve poisons and intoxicants consists not only in their immediate psychological and physical effects but also in the period during which they can be used or abused before addiction supervenes.

*While it is possible to become a heroinist or cocainist within a week, it takes perhaps a couple of weeks to become a morphinist, some months of abuse to be a barbiturate or amphetamine addict, and generally three to ten years to be an alcoholic, after heavy drinking within the social norms of Western society.* It is, however, important to know that the younger the abuser the more rapidly dependence develops.

Hashish dependence develops far more rapidly than alcohol dependence. After only a few months of intensive abuse it seems to be very difficult for the individual to break the habit. The cannabis dependent person is able to discontinue his drug consumption for short periods, but if the preparation is easily available there is a very strong tendency to relapse. The price cannabis smokers are prepared to pay and the considerable legal

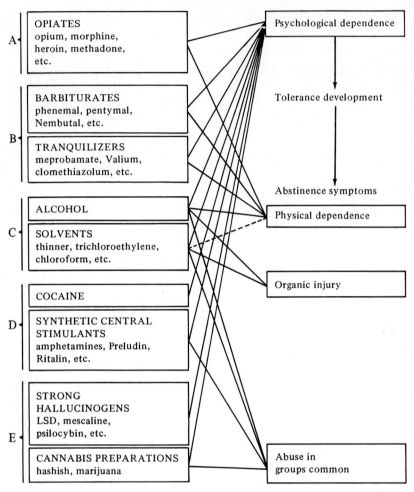

Figure 2. Survey of various groups of addicting substances and different types of dependence (modified model from Mogens Jacobsen).

risks he is prepared to take in many countries is to some extent an objective measure of the strength of his dependence.

## LEGISLATION

It is to some extent the very varying risks for the development of dependence which explains why legislation differs so much in regard to different drugs.

It is not possible to control all addicting substances by means of legislation, least of all the solvents required for technical and industrial use. *Legislation should therefore also be directed to the condition of the addict and his need for medical attention, and not only to the chemical nature of the drug.*

# Chapter 3

# WHICH ROADS LEAD TO ADDICTION?

**B**EFORE we go into the question of who runs the greatest risk of being drawn into addiction, we will take a look at the usual paths into addiction.

Before 1965, addictions were classified only according to the type of drug abused, and addicts were described as morphinists, heroinists, amphetaminists etc. In that year I introduced a socio-medical classification and divided addictions into single, epidemic, and endemic types.

### SINGLE CASES

By single cases is meant addictions which have arisen without the influence of other addicts. We can distinguish three main types of single cases:

1. *Addiction consciously accepted during medical treatment.* This is mainly a matter of the relief of pain in incurable and dying patients, and a complicating addiction in these cases has to be accepted. Generally there is no great problem with regard to these addictions.

2. *Addictions inadvertently caused by medical treatment.* Isolated cases of morphinism have arisen in this way. Experience from World War II shows, however, that the risk of addiction is small in correct medical treatment of pain.

On the other hand, it is not unusual for nervous and anxiety-ridden patients to become addicted through overdosing of tranquilizing drugs and sleeping tablets. The risk is particularly great if the patients wander from one physician to another, and receive drugs here and there without any coordination of the medication.

3. *Self-established addictions.* These are old and familiar phenomena. Through the ease with which they can obtain drugs, medical staff have always run a risk through self-administration of dangerous drugs in conditions of pain, depression, or stress.

30

*In none of these three groups of single cases is there any marked tendency to draw others into drug abuse.* The individual cases are often very severe, but they are not *contagious*—with some reservation for addicted physicians, about a fifth of whom draw their wives into addiction, and have a marked tendency to be careless in prescribing dangerous drugs to patients.

## EPIDEMIC ADDICTIONS

It is often considered that some kind of microbes are involved if we talk of epidemics. Other forms of contagion occur, however. We had, for instance, bizarre mass phenomena during the Middle Ages, such as epidemics of dancing. Local outbreaks of suicide and arson occur now and then.

The literature abounds in descriptions of small, local, mental epidemics, and I will quote a recent report from Britain (Benaim, Horder and Anderson, 1971):

> An epidemic of falling, confined to one single class of a large comprehensive school in a London Suburb, is described. There were 24 adolescent girls in the class, all in the sixteen-seventeen age group, and the class was involved in examinations. The school authorities decided to close down the class one week before the end of term, when 8 girls and a young locum teacher lay unconscious on the floor. Most of the girls affected belonged to the "in-group": the very bright, the Greek, the Jewish and the 1 coloured girl were unaffected.

One of the protagonists of the epidemic was admitted to hospital for observation, and there she started a hysterical "pregnancy epidemic" in her ward.

The epidemic addictions have a number of characteristics which differentiate them radically from addictions of single type. I will briefly describe eleven of the most important peculiarities of addiction of epidemic type.

1. *Contagion. The type of epidemic addiction which now afflicts most Western industrial countries has as a prerequisite, direct, personal contagion between an established abuser and a beginner.* No one can learn to inject drugs into the veins unless he has been taught by an experienced person. It is perhaps less widely recognized that you cannot even learn to smoke hashish properly without being taught the technique.

Contagion in epidemic addictions is spread almost exclusively via close personal contact. It is a common misconception that pushers initiate people into abuse of this type. Pushers come into the picture later and they then play a pernicious role as suppliers and reinforcers.

2.   *Rapid spread.* The number of single cases in a society is usually fairly constant, while *drug epidemics, when conditions are unchanged, seem to develop by geometric progression.* The heroin epidemic in Britain doubled every sixteenth month between 1959-67 (Bewley 1968). The Swedish amphetamine epidemic doubled every thirtieth month from 1948-68 (Bejerot 1970). This development was temporarily checked in 1969 by a tremendous police offensive on the drug trade.

3.   *Historic boundaries.* The epidemic addictions always start suddenly, as when a spark lights a forest fire. On the other hand, it may smoulder in the undergrowth a long while before the flames break out in full force.

Drug epidemics may be brought to an end, as the great amphetamine epidemic in Japan after the World War II, or the Chinese opium smoking, which was checked by drastic action after the revolution in 1949. The cocaine epidemics in England and Germany in the twenties were also checked by legal methods.

4.   *Geographic boundaries.* The epidemic may be limited to a school, a district in a city, a region, or a country. On the other hand, the epidemic addictions are checked by political and geographical boundaries even if communications across the borders are lively.

For example, before December 1966 the Danish authorities did not know of any intravenous addicts. Swedish peddlers had made energetic attempts to sell central stimulants in Copenhagen, but failed completely until 1967. In the early months of 1968, there was already a daughter epidemic of a few hundred cases of intravenous abuse in Copenhagen, and one year later there were an estimated 500 cases. In the late autumn 1971 there were about 3,500 intravenous drug abusers in Denmark, mainly teenagers, and most of them were using opiates (morphine base).

5.   *Ethnic boundaries.* For a long time foreign citizenship gave

almost complete protection from being drawn into intravenous drug abuse even for people living in the middle of Stockholm, the center of the Swedish epidemic.

In 1965 there was a breakthrough into the large Finnish population in Stockholm. In 1966 a daughter epidemic broke out in Helsinki also.

The first cases of intravenous abuse were reported from Norway in 1967, and some other individual foreigners have also learned the injection technique in Sweden and then returned to their home countries.

Also, in the little epidemic of falling girls described on page 31 the ethnic boundaries were strong enough to protect the non-Anglian girls although they attended the same school class.

6. *Age distribution.* The epidemics first affect narrow age groups. Thinner sniffing usually occurs in young teenagers; hashish smoking in the upper teens and the early twenties; intravenous drug abuse originally spread among 25 to 30 year olds.

The more a drug epidemic spreads, the broader the age distribution becomes. In the spring of 1965 there were very few persons under 20 or over 40 who took drugs intravenously in the Stockholm arrest population. And yet at that time 39 percent of the arrestees between 25 and 30 were injecting drugs.

*The rates for this advanced form of abuse in the youngest and oldest age groups in the arrest population (those between 15-20 and 40-45) increased tenfold between spring 1965 and spring 1967—from 3 percent to 30 percent.*

7. *Characteristic sex ratios.* While the proportion of men to women is usually about 1:1 in addiction of therapeutic type (women may even be overrepresented in this group), men are always very overrepresented in addiction of epidemic type. The male excess tends, however, to diminish the more widely spread the epidemic becomes and the older it grows.

In the beginning of a drug epidemic there are often six to eight men to every woman involved, but the difference falls successively to three or four men to every woman (heroinism in the United States and England, amphetamine abuse in Japan and Sweden, use of alcohol in the Muhammadan part of the world). If a drug epidemic finally becomes an endemic and socially accepted phenomenon the proportion of women increases successively (as, for instance, in the use of tobacco and alcohol in industrial countries), but only exceptionally seems to reach the proportions 1:1. This, however, appears to have happened among coca-chewing Indian tribes in South America.

8. *Group boundaries.* Hashish smoking was brought to Scandinavia by American *jazz musicians* in the late forties. For a long while hashish was confined to just these circles in Scandinavia.

In 1965 there were about 200 hashish smokers in Sweden, nearly all in Stockholm, and centered around one jazz restaurant. Four years later there were tens of thousands of *school children and students* all over the country who had tried hashish, and it is now impossible to estimate the number who are severely addicted. The pop music culture played an important role in spreading the cannabis cult in Scandinavia.

Intravenous drug abuse, on the other hand, represents quite another epidemic and affects different groups; until 1965 mainly criminals.

9. *Massivity.* Drug abuse, as opposed to addiction, is often a symptom of maladjustment of various kinds. This is particularly the case when the drugs cannot be obtained legally. It is often deviating individuals who are prepared to engage in criminal activity in order to obtain drugs for which, in the beginning, they have no craving; and it is the maladjusted youth who form the core of most new drug epidemics. It should be remembered, however, that many youths start on drugs during a critical phase in what might otherwise have been a normal course of development; also when addicts are asked why it was that they took the first dose, the reason most commonly given is that it was out of curiosity or the desire to belong to an "in-group."

The more widespread abuse becomes, the less predisposing personality disorders and social difficulties are required for an individual to be drawn in. This corresponds to the massivity phenomenon in epidemics spread by microbes. If, for instance, the concentration of pathogenic bacteria in a room is low it is possible that none of the people there will catch the disease, although they have all been in contact with the bacteria and inhaled them. If the concentration of bacteria (massivity) is raised, the weakest in the group will ultimately be infected, the weakest here meaning the one with the greatest susceptibility. If the concentration of bacteria is further increased, for instance because a large number of those present have caught the disease, it will finally reach such a massivity that even the strongest in the group, the one with the greatest power of resistance, may be infected.

This mechanism has been exemplified very clearly in the present cannabis epidemic where, after a time, large groups of ordinary youth have been drawn in through the massivity effect in their environment.

10. *Sensitivity to fashion in choice of drugs.* Abuse of central stimulants began in Sweden at the end of the forties with amphetamine. During 1957-58 the new slimming drug Preludin (phenmetrazine) came into the picture and took the place of amphetamine. For a period Ritalin (methylphenidate) was very popular. When Preludin was taken off the legal market amphetamine, illicitly manufactured, came back into fashion .

11. *Sensitivity to fashion for method of administration.* For a long while the tablets were taken orally in addict circles in Sweden. At the end of the forties, addicts began to dissolve the drugs and inject them directly into the veins. At the end of the sixties there were not many addicts who were content to take the drugs by mouth.

In America, subcutaneous injections of opiates was for a long period the usual method of administration. After World War II the intravenous technique was adopted by almost all heroinists in the United States. In Hong Kong people still smoke opiates, even though it is usually heroin they smoke these days.

*In comparison with single cases, the epidemic addictions constitute quite a different form of illness—even if the addicts are dependent upon the same drug. The really serious factor is that all addicts of epidemic type are potentially contagious.*

## Comparison Between Addictions of Single and Epidemic Type

The epidemic model represents a social dynamic approach to youth addictions in contrast to the traditional model, drug-

TABLE I

SOME CONTRASTS IN TWO TYPES OF OPIATE DEPENDENCE

from H. Brill (1968).

| *Characteristic* | *Nonmedical (Street Addict)* | *Medical* |
|---|---|---|
| Usual age range of cases | 18 to 30 (avg. 27). | 30 and beyond (avg. 40). |
| Male/female ratio | 6 or 8 men to each woman. | Female incidence equals that of male. |
| Locale | Cases tightly clustered in specific metropolitan areas. | Cases dispersed. |
| Drugs used | Heroin is the drug of choice; multiple drug use is the rule, marijuana frequent. | Morphine and demerol the prevailing drugs; heroin rare in U. S., infrequent abroad. |
| Psychiatric classification | Character and personality disorders. | Neuroses, depressions, and psychoses; psychosomatic disorders. |
| Psychiatric history | Conduct disorder only. | Long history of subjective symptoms, often psychosomatic. |
| Severity of habit | Fluctuating but characteristically severe. | Varies in severity; unknown proportion of cases thought to follow stable dosage. |
| Degree of economic disability | Severe as a rule often to the point of vagabondage (periodic). | Serious but often not complete; many retain a degree of marginal productivity. |
| Effect of maturation | A proportion of cases recover as they age (loss of capacity for euphoric reaction?). | Probably not a factor. |
| Condition after drug withdrawal is completed | Marked physical and mental improvement is the rule. | An underlying psychiatric disturbance may be uncovered or existing one increase in severity. |
| Delinquency | Frequent before, and during addiction; also seen after. | Delinquency not a feature prior to addiction; tends to be limited to technical infractions during addiction. |
| Way in which habit began | Usually "on the street" under social pressure of a group and seeking pleasure. | Under medical conditions. For treatment of a complaint. |
| Social use of drugs | Frequent use in groups. | Solitary use only. |
| Psychic contagion | Primary mode of spread. May assume epidemic proportions. | Not a problem. |
| Attitude toward drug use | Often seen as highly desirable. | Guilt and anxiety. |

individual-milieu, which is more static and does not allow differentiation between the main social medical types of addiction.

As the epidemic terminology may seem confusing, I will point out that in epidemic addiction it is the drug-taking behavior—not the drug—which corresponds to microbes in infectious diseases and is responsible for transmission of addiction.

Several other authors have differentiated two main types of addiction along roughly the same lines as my single and epidemic cases. The sociologist Lindesmith (U. S.) talks of addiction of the "old" and "new" type. Bewley (England) describes "therapeutic" and "nontherapeutic" addicts, and James (England) uses the addicts' own terminology, "junkies," for epidemic cases.

Brill (U. S.) has gone further and classified the differences between what he describes as "nonmedical or street addicts" and "medical addicts" (Table I). Brill notes the contagious nature of nonmedical addiction, the characteristic to which I have attributed the nucleus of the problem.

Apart from various types of single cases and the epidemic forms we have still another main category of addiction.

## ENDEMIC ADDICTIONS

These are addictions which are constantly present in a country and which have arisen as a result of a more or less socially accepted use of certain addicting substances used for enjoyment, relaxation, or stimulation. Presumably endemic addictions often began as epidemics which continually gained ground and eventually, evolved to allow the drug abuse to become socially accepted. It is possible that we are witnessing today the conversion of a marijuana epidemic into an endemic in the United States.

Among endemic addictions we can include opium smoking in ancient China, hashish smoking in North Africa, and coca chewing among South American Indians. In principle, of course, alcoholism is an endemic addiction also. It exists mainly in the Christian parts of the world, while Buddhist and Muhammadan countries have been spared alcoholism thanks to their religious precepts. It appears that Muhammad not only eradicated alcoholism in North Africa and Asia Minor, but also the grapevine.

Since endemic forms of addiction arise on the basis of the drug being more or less socially tolerated within the country, these addictions affect a more average and "normal" selection of the population than the epidemic addictions. Epidemic addictions mainly affect special population groups (youth, bohemians, criminals etc.).

These phenomena can be clearly seen in Sweden. Alcoholism, our endemic form of addiction, affects the various population groups fairly evenly. The intravenous abuse, on the other hand, which has a markedly epidemic character, affects very deviated groups.

## Chapter 4

# WHO BECOMES ADDICTED?

W E HAVE already pointed out that those who are first drawn into a mass addiction are maladjusted persons, usually people with deep psychological disturbances and an unfavorable social background.

This has been demonstrated for American heroinists, Swedish thinner sniffers, and also for Swedish addicts of the intravenous type. When the mass abuse becomes more widespread, less and less deviating persons are drawn into the risk zone, and finally just ordinary people are drawn in. There is plenty of proof of this development.

Most of the first *Swedish morphinists of gang type* were homosexuals. By means of morphine they dampened their deviating sexual desires, and at the same time achieved a kind of sexual surrogate from the strong pleasurable sensations experienced on intravenous injection of opiates. Later these pleasurable sensations are reduced and finally, in many cases, almost disappear and leave only discomfort and distress. The first Swedish addicts taking central stimulants intravenously were all very disturbed persons. After the initial bohemian phase the epidemic spread almost exclusively in criminal circles until the middle of the sixties.

If we follow the development of jaundice (which in this connection arises from transmission of a particular virus, usually through contaminated syringes and needles), we see that in the beginning the disease affected people who had a massive criminal background. Now it largely affects youth, and even adults, who were previously unknown to the police.

*Cannabis smoking* affects ordinary youth to an even greater extent. Hashish smokers, more than the average youth, have had problems with themselves and their environment. But to try and explain the rapid spread of the epidemic of cannabis smoking on

39

the basis of theories of individual psychology is doomed to failure. Since the days of Adam and Eve men have blamed their sins and failures on the female; but just as it is difficult to see any sudden deterioration in the social conditions in Sweden in the sixties—and in Denmark in the last few years—so is it unlikely that we would find any sudden increase in the number of unaffectionate or overprotective mothers now or 15 to 20 years ago when these young addicts were born.

These theories tend to produce a feeling of inferiority in the addicts and of guilt in their parents. The argument is also unfruitful and does not give any practical indications as to how the problem should be brought under control. On the contrary, the individual psychology approach seems to paralyze society and produce a feeling of hopelessness and powerlessness in the face of the mass addiction: "There is so little we can do."

A Swedish investigation (Jonsson-Kälvesten 1964) showed that in a random sample of school boys in Stockholm, a quarter needed psychiatric treatment. Similar investigations among adults have shown that the need for psychiatric treatment is of the same dimensions there.

In all societies there is a very large group of people who are potential risks in regard to drug abuse and addiction. Experience shows that prevention must primarily be directed towards eliminating drugs from society, and secondarily to preventing spread of addiction by removing addicts of epidemic type from the epidemic dynamics.

A question commonly asked is why certain persons continue to take drugs instead of stopping after trying them out. This question is wrongly framed from a biological approach. From animal experiments we know that the normal pattern is to continue with pleasurable stimulation when it has once been experienced. If we apply this argument to humans it would mean that it is *natural to continue drug consumption and to stop is deviant behaviour* (deviant from the basic biological pattern). On the other hand, if we ask what it is that makes some people discontinue drug consumption or keep it at a low level and under control, we will get an instructive answer, which suggests that information, knowledge, attitudes, personality, social background, the current situation and above all, social control, play a decisive role in the *initial phase*—before the craving for the drug has taken on the character of a basic drive.

It is essential to bear in mind that *the reason why people start taking drugs is quite different from the reason why they continue*: they represent in principle quite different problems, rather like the causes of fires and inflammability are two completely different questions.

## Chapter 5

# SYMPTOMS OF DRUG ABUSE

THE ADVANCED abuse of drugs—regardless of what drugs are used—causes such great changes in the physical, psychological, and social conditions of the addict that he cannot conceal his situation from his family. As a rule the relations between the addict and his family become strained to the breaking point; but even in those cases where relations are good all the time the addicts show a marked tendency to make little of their dependence even to those nearest to them, and to understate the quantity of drugs consumed. Also, they often blame their drug abuse on external circumstances or on pain, worry, and so on.

It is very difficult to recognize the symptoms of early drug abuse, and these symptoms are also difficult to interpret. The first alarm signal is usually a relatively rapid change in the behavior and habits of the individual. Previously well-behaved youth may suddenly begin to stay out late; they usually lose interest in school or work, have difficulty in getting up in the mornings, become irritable and short tempered etc.

I must add at once that in most cases where teenagers behave in this way it is, fortunately, not a question of drug abuse, but a crisis in development, and usually they mature and become stable again.

If drugs are being abused there is, as a rule, a continued deterioration of the psychological and social situation. If an individual has commenced taking *intravenous injections* it is only a matter of time before the relatives notice blood stains on his shirt sleeves (at the elbow), find blood-stained pieces of cotton wool, and sooner or later, even syringes and needles, the latter often behind the lapel of a jacket. Also, the needle marks at the inside of the elbow joint and on the forearms (sometimes on the inside of the upper arm) are very reliable signs of drug abuse.

It is also possible from behavior, movements, and the play of the features, to see if a person is under the influence of central stimulants; he is usually talkative, his thoughts are scattered. On strong intoxication his movements are jerky and his face may sometimes be distorted by spasmodic, unmotivated, and uncontrollable grimaces.

The *cannabis smoker* may also possess some utensils which are characteristic: Hashish is smoked in a pipe, and it is usually cut up into small pieces, so a sharp knife is required. If the individual is a peddler himself he usually has a little pair of letter scales, often pocket size. Hashish for daily use is often kept in match boxes.

The hashish smoker likes to arrange an undisturbed corner for himself and his friends, and he appreciates dim lights and an atmopshere of calm and mystery. The strong, sweet smell of hashish is clear evidence of smoking.

The intoxicated hashish smoker is given to giggling and unmotivated laughter. Behavior similar to drunkeness but without alcohol or thinner smell is very suspicious of cannabis intoxication. Intensive smoking may cause a slight reddening of the whites of the eyes and catarrhal symptoms, but these are very uncertain signs of intensive consumption.

There is an altered attitude to life and a tendency towards quasi-philosophical speculation and mysticism, but this occurs at a relatively late stage in intensive abuse of cannabis. As logical thought is affected, a tendency to magical ways of thinking develops. We often see, therefore, a deep interest in astrology and a strong fixation to magical insignia in the heavy hashish smoker.

Chapter 6

# DRUG EPIDEMICS

THE DRAMATIC history of drug epidemics does not support the theory that the phenomenon of mass addiction is a symptom of psychological or social maladjustment. If individual maladjustment was the dominant factor leading to addiction, we would expect to find a fairly stable drug situation in most countries. Social conditions change very slowly except in certain definite situations such as revolution and war. There is no evidence to suggest that there are any great, sudden changes in the prevalence of neuroses, family conflicts, unloving parents and so on, in societies with widespread drug epidemics. In contrast to the slow changes in the mental health situation of a nation, drug abuse flares up suddenly in a society and spreads very rapidly, and these drug epidemics have no constant coincidence with periods of revolution, war, economic depression etc. If social conditions such as bad housing and low wages were a cause of addiction, it is difficult to explain why epidemic addictions affect three to eight times as many men as women. The women live in the same houses as the men and their wages are usually lower. Among cases of therapeutic addiction the women are always at least as numerous as the men. The first addiction epidemic in modern time arose in Ireland at the beginning of the nineteenth century and even spread to England, Germany, and France. Tens of thousands of persons began to abuse a new chemical substance used in industry. The mass abuse could not be stopped until restrictions were imposed on the sale of the substance. This illustrates the decisive role of availability of drugs in maintaining an epidemic.

At the end of World War II, Japan was afflicted by a wave of addiction of the same type (amphetamine) as in Sweden today. At the close of hostilities the military supply of amphetamines fell into wrong hands. Addiction spread first among prostitutes and criminals, later in wider circles.

44

After the war, central stimulants were sold freely in Japan. Production of the drug increased and the authorities were soon forced to put amphetamines on prescription and later to class them as dangerous drugs. By then, however, the avalanche was on the move. Tens of thousands had become addicted, and widespread illegal manufacture, smuggling, and trade had taken the place of the legal drug market.

When the epidemic culminated in 1954, an estimated two million of Japan's population of 100 million had abused amphetamine at some time or other. It was determined that 600,000 were then severe amphetaminists, and half of them injected the drug intravenously.

The situation was extremely alarming. A number of countermeasures were introduced from 1949 and onwards, but they were not far-reaching enough, and as in Sweden, the steps taken were commenced too late. The counterattack the whole time lay one stage behind the development of the epidemic.

In 1954 a strong public opinion developed in Japan against the extensive drug abuse which, at that time, was far more widespread than the Swedish epidemic has ever been. Legislation was sharpened drastically and the raw material used in the manufacture of amphetamines was brought under the same strict control as amphetamine itself. The Japanese had not had time to build up any treatment centers, and the penal services had to take care of all those proved to have had illicit dealings with drugs.

For cases of illicit possession of small quantities of the drug the punishment was three to six months imprisonment, for minor peddling one to two years, for trading in illicit drugs two to four years, and for illegal manufacture and large-scale smuggling up to ten years.

In 1954, 55,600 persons were arrested for drug crimes in Japan, but in 1958 the figure was down to 271, and the epidemic was over. Some of the drug abusers went over to alcohol, but the great majority returned to a drug-free life.

Since then, drug abuse in Japan has been of insignificant proportions. There was a small epidemic of heroin abuse in the early sixties which affected a few thousand individuals. This was quickly brought under control, however, in the same way as the amphetamine epidemic. At the end of the sixties there has been a certain amount of abuse of sleeping tablets for which no prescriptions were required, and thinner sniffing has also occurred, but the rates have been low.

Today, Japan is the only industrial country outside Eastern Europe which has avoided the violent cannabis epidemics which have swept over the whole of the Western world since the middle of the sixties. It appears that Japan has learned empirically how to stop addiction epidemics, and the Japanese have understood the decisive importance of early and consistent countermeasures.

In Eastern Europe the authorities have always been as well-prepared as in Japan. Illicit possession of narcotic drugs is more severely punished in the Soviet Union than in most other countries. In the early fifties the People's Republic of China started a campaign against the centuries-old opium smoking, and this was as hard, dramatic, and successful as the Japanese attack on amphetamine. It is possible, and even probable, that the Japanese benefited from the Chinese success in this field.

## EXPERIENCE FROM ENGLAND

At the end of the fifties a few British physicians began to experiment with liberal prescriptions of narcotic drugs to addicts of epidemic type. They hoped that the addicts would then be independent of the illegal market and thus could break away from the criminal life which was often necessary if they were to finance their expensive illicit drug purchase. This treatment was possible because of the permissive British legislation, introduced by a Tory government in 1926, which gave every physician a free hand to treat his patients according to his own judgment and in a way which his own experience and ideas had convinced him was most suitable.

Half a dozen Canadian heroinists emigrated to England in 1959 as a British psychiatrist, Lady Frankau, promised to treat them and prescribe heroin for them. The first year, optimistic reports were published which declared that several of these chronic heroinists had settled down in a socially useful life once their need of heroin had been satisfied through cheap supplies from the chemist shops. Many experienced psychiatrists with long practice in addiction treatment pointed out that this treatment contained a number of hazards which were difficult to control. They recalled the similar treatment experiment in the United States in the twenties which had proved a failure, and they were not inclined to support the practice. The favorable primary results, however, gave the supporters of the system confidence, and the method came to be called "the British system" in the scientific and popular press.

Soon, disturbing tendencies were observed in connection with the permissive prescribing of narcotic drugs in England. It was found that addicts undergoing this treatment were providing other people with the prescribed drugs on a rather large scale. The drugs were "lent" or more often sold at a very high profit. Developments became more and more disturbing, and during 1964 and 1965 there were alarming reports in the British medical press. Chapple and Marks wrote the following (1965):

> It has been discovered that one of our patients has made at least 11 persons into heroinists while he was under treatment with legal prescriptions from his own doctor; these 11 are now "legalized addicts" and are probably extending the abuse to others. We consider that no further prescribing of heroin to new addicts should be allowed, and the legal prescriptions in the cases now receiving them should be "frozen" and reduced.

The prescriptions often took the form of standing orders for certain quantities which could be collected daily.

Many addicts in England lived in comfort and leisure on the proceeds of their legal prescriptions. James (1965) mentions that "a supply of gr.10 of heroin and gr.5 of cocaine per day has a market value of over £100 per week." Glatt (1965) summarized his opinion of the much-discussed "British system" by saying: "But a system which is respected by neither general practitioners, hospitals, addicts, nor parents of addicts can hardly be called a good one."

The alarming development in England was demonstrated in

## TABLE II

### HOME OFFICE REPORT OF ADDICTS ON DANGEROUS DRUGS

| Drug Addicts | 1958 | 1959 | 1960 | 1961 | 1962 | 1963 | 1964 | 1965 | 1966 | 1967 | 1968 |
|---|---|---|---|---|---|---|---|---|---|---|---|
| TOTAL NUMBER | 442 | 454 | 437 | 470 | 532 | 635 | 753 | 927 | 1349 | 1729 | 2782 |
| **DRUGS*** | | | | | | | | | | | |
| No. taking morphine | 205 | 204 | 177 | 168 | 157 | 172 | 162 | 160 | 178 | 158 | 198 |
| No. taking heroin | 62 | 68 | 94 | 132 | 175 | 237 | 342 | 521 | 899 | 1299 | 2240 |
| No. taking cocaine | 25 | 30 | 52 | 84 | 112 | 171 | 211 | 311 | 443 | 462 | 564 |
| No. taking Pethidine | 117 | 116 | 98 | 105 | 112 | 107 | 128 | 102 | 131 | 112 | 120 |
| **ORIGIN** | | | | | | | | | | | |
| No. of therapeutic origin | 349 | 344 | 309 | 293 | 312 | 355 | 368 | 344 | 351 | 313 | 306 |
| No. of non-therapeutic origin | 68 | 98 | 122 | 159 | 212 | 270 | 372 | 580 | 982 | 1385 | 2420 |
| No. of unknown origin | 25 | 12 | 6 | 18 | 8 | 10 | 13 | 3 | 16 | 31 | 56 |
| **AGES** | | | | | | | | | | | |
| Under 20 | — | — | 1 | 2 | 3 | 17 | 40 | 145 | 329 | 395 | 764 |
| Under 20 taking heroin | — | — | 1 | 2 | 3 | 17 | 40 | 134 | 317 | 381 | 709 |
| 20-34 | — | 50 | 62 | 94 | 132 | 184 | 257 | 347 | 558 | 906 | 1530 |
| 20-34 taking heroin | — | 35 | 52 | 87 | 126 | 162 | 219 | 319 | 479 | 827 | 1390 |
| 35-49 | — | 92 | 91 | 95 | 107 | 128 | 138 | 134 | 162 | 142 | 146 |
| 35-49 taking heroin | — | 7 | 14 | 19 | 24 | 38 | 61 | 52 | 83 | 66 | 78 |
| 50 and over | — | 278 | 267 | 272 | 274 | 298 | 311 | 291 | 286 | 279 | 260 |
| 50 and over taking heroin | — | 26 | 27 | 24 | 22 | 20 | 22 | 16 | 20 | 24 | 20 |
| Age unknown | — | 34 | 16 | 7 | 16 | 8 | 7 | 10 | 14 | 7 | 82 |
| Age unknown taking heroin | — | — | — | — | — | — | — | — | — | 1 | 43 |

| SEX** | | | | | | | | | | |
|---|---|---|---|---|---|---|---|---|---|---|
| No. of male addicts | 197 | 196 | 195 | 223 | 262 | 339 | 409 | 558 | 886 | 1262 | 2161 |
| No. of female addicts | 245 | 258 | 242 | 247 | 270 | 296 | 344 | 369 | 463 | 467 | 621 |

PROFESSIONAL CLASSES

| (Medical or allied) Total number | 74 | 68 | 63 | 61 | 57 | 56 | 58 | 45 | 54 | 56 | 43 |
|---|---|---|---|---|---|---|---|---|---|---|---|

*The figures refer to drugs used alone or in combination with other drugs. Thus, an addict using both heroin and cocaine will be included under both drugs, and it must be pointed out that all but a handful of the cocaine addicts shown above are also using heroin.

**Before 1959 the addicts in England were almost entirely of therapeutic or iatrogenic type. In addictions of this type, women are always as many or even more numerous than the men. When the epidemic of heroin addiction began to expand, the picture was soon altered and male abusers began to dominate.

figures by the interdepartmental committee, the so-called Brain Committee, which in its report (1965) showed that heroinism in the most active abuse ages (between 20 and 35) had increased by 50 percent each year since 1959, when the liberal policy of prescribing drugs to addicts was first practiced in England on a wide scale. Bewley (1968) showed that the rate of recording new cases of heroinism had been doubled every 16 months in the preceding ten years. The official figures from the Home Office are given in Table II. The British authorities are now trying desperately to gain control over this heroin epidemic for which a handful of injudicious physicians bear much of the blame through their ignorance and abuse of a far too permissive legislation. The law is now changed, and private practitioners may no longer prescribe heroin and cocaine, but they may prescribe morphine, methadone and amphetamine on the same premises as previously. The majority of the addicts have been transferred to special narcotic clinics, but the situation is extremely precarious. When the manufacturers drastically reduced deliveries of amphetamine to the chemist shops many addicts of epidemic type began to go over to intravenous abuse of barbiturates, which is the same phenomena that has been observed in Sweden.

In England the social psychiatrist R. de Alarcón has demonstrated the pattern of spread in the heroin epidemic. He has drawn up an interesting diagram regarding a careful study in Crawley (62,000 inhabitants), a new town just outside London (Fig. 3).

The material is based on interviews with heroinists found in a careful case-finding study. The patients were asked when they had received their first injection, who had given it to them, and also who they themselves had initiated.

Altogether the study involved 53 boys and five girls, all between 15 and 20. Forty-two of the youngsters gave the approximate date of the first injection and the name of the initiator. In 16 of these the information was verified by the initiator himself. Eight refused to disclose the name of their initiators, but mentioned when they had been initiated (cases A1, C1, E1, F1, H1, I1 and J1). Four of these (A1, C1, D1 and

E1) stated that they had been initiated in another town. Seven cases (A7, A25, A26, B5, B10, B12 and B14) were mentioned by the initiators alone.

Alarcón divides the pattern of spread into three stages:

1. *1962-65.* A few Crawley youth experimented with heroin while staying temporally in other towns. The period between the first injection and regular abuse was long—up to one year.

2. *The first half of 1966.* A nucleus of young heroinists was formed in Crawley. Not all of them acted as "initiators" but most of them acted as "reinforcers."

3. *The second half of 1966 and the first half of 1967.* The population at risk was in contact with a large number of "initiators" and "reinforcers," and heroin abuse developed explosively in the community. The period between initiation and regular abuse was short.

The spread of contagion was along two main channels (A and B). During 1965 and 1966 legal prescribing of heroin to established addicts was practiced, but this was stopped by the new legislation in 1967. Alarcón wrote "Preliminary data suggest that the figure for 1968 will show a marked decline in the

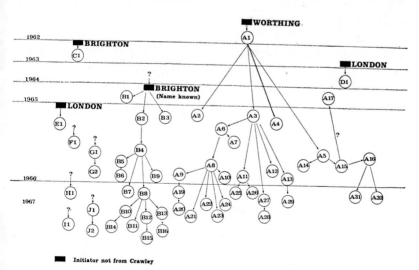

Figure 3. Spread of heroin abuse in Crawley, England. (Material from de Alarcón)

number of new cases of heroin abuse in Crawley." He calculates that legislation against the prescribing of heroin to addicts may be the most important cause of the decline in new cases. Other factors are the migration of the most severe cases—and worst sources of contagion—to London, and the change over from heroin to central stimulants in the new addict circles in Crawley. Alarcón stresses that drug dependence is a chronic disease. Only three of the youngsters in this survey are known to have discontinued their drug abuse after taking the first injection.

## EXPERIENCE FROM SWEDEN

Amphetamines were first used clinically shortly before World War II. Some tendency to abuse the drugs was observed early in other countries, particularly among students who took stimulants when they were studying for exams. Reasonable doses bring about some increases in both physical and mental capacity, but self-criticism is reduced and judgment blunted. Even memory deteriorates under the influence of these drugs. During World War II most combatant countries probably used amphetamines on a large scale in order to temporarily stimulate exhausted soldiers during long and trying operations.

The Swedish abuse of central stimulants may be traced back to a little group of authors, actors, and painters at the end of the forties. The epidemic was for a long while contained within this narrow circle where the injection technique was also initiated. Amphetamine abuse spread to asocial and criminally active circles in Stockholm in the early fifties.

Intravenous drug abuse spread successively, but up to 1956 it was confined to Stockholm. In that year a severely addicted teenaged boy moved to Gothenburg and started the first drug den there, and until his death in 1968 he was a leading figure in addict circles in the city.

The Swedish epidemic appears to have increased by geometric progression and doubled roughly every thirtieth month up to 1965, when there were an estimated 4,000 addicts, mainly in the Stockholm area.

During the fifties, supplies of central stimulants were obtained from careless prescribing of slimming pills by unsuspecting physicians. When abuse of these drugs became generally evident, prescribing of central stimulants was restricted, and from the end of the fifties supplies were obtained almost entirely through a widespread smuggling from southern Europe where these drugs could be bought freely even in the early seventies.

Up to the beginning of 1965 the Swedish narcotic drug policy had been traditionally cautious and restrictive. Early in 1965 a little vociferous group of laymen, supported by a couple of physicians, started a campaign for a permissive drug policy. A violent public opinion developed, and within a few months, in the spring of 1965, the Board of Health agreed to sanction an "experiment" with liberal prescribing of drugs to addicts for self-administration.

A few physicians then commenced prescribing central stimulants, and also opiates, to addicts of epidemic type. The most active physician prescribed to an average of 82 patients during two years no less than 600,000 standard doses of opiates and 4 million doses of central stimulants. In the beginning his patients received an average of 1,000 doses per person and month, after six months they were up in 2,000 doses, and when the activity was stopped in May 1967, they were receiving an average of 3,000 doses per person and month. The prescribed drugs were sold widely on the black market, and an interview study among arrestees showed that every fourth drug abuser had obtained drugs from someone he knew to be in receipt of these prescriptions.

From a continuous study of the addiction rates among arrestees in Stockholm, I was able to show that the epidemic doubled during only twelve months in direct connection with this experiment in 1965-1967 with permissive prescribing practice (Bejerot 1970).

Since April 1965, with the help of trained nurses, I have followed intravenous drug abuse in Stockholm in the arrest population through examination of arms for needle marks. The results of the injection mark study have proved remarkably representative. In the second half of 1967, the National Drug Dependence Committee carried out a large-scale case-finding study of drug abusers known in the Greater Stockholm area.

For this the Committee mobilized the whole of the health service apparatus, the social welfare organizations, the school authorities, police, penal services etc. and a total of 1,949 active intravenous addicts were reported. Of these no less than 70 percent were known in the injection mark study (Fig. 4). A

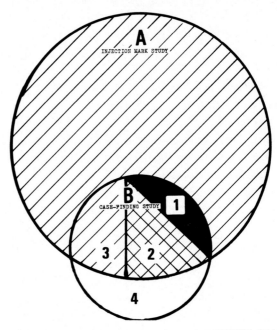

Figure 4. RELATIONS BETWEEN THE INJECTION MARK STUDY AND THE CASE-FINDING STUDY:

    A. The injection mark study (IMS) April 1965-June 1969.

    B. Case-finding study (CFS) in Greater Stockholm, July 1-December 31, 1967 (1,949 individuals = 100%).

    1. Cases exclusively reported from the IMS during the case-finding period (333 cases = 17.1%).

    2. Cases reported from the IMS and another source in the CFS during the case-finding period (459 cases = 23.6%).

    3. Cases in the CFS reported from another source than the IMS but known as abusers of intravenous type in the IMS 1965-1969 (579 cases = 29.7%).

    4. Cases unknown in the IMS 1965-1969 (578 cases = 29.7%).

The figures and percentages apply to men and women together (Swedish citizens).

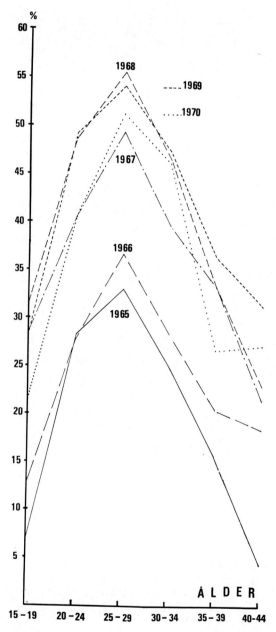

Figure 5. Percentage of drug abuse of intravenuos type in different age groups among male Swedes arrested under the criminal code in Stockholm, April 1965 to June 1970.

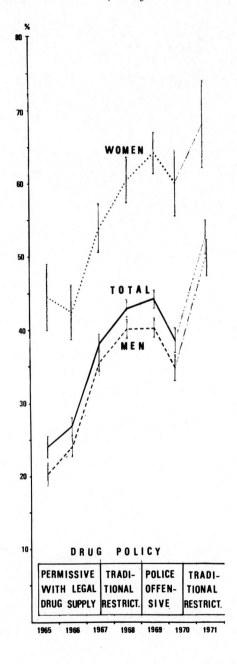

considerable number of those who were not known in this study were young abusers, and experience shows that many of them will later be observed in the injection mark study.

Up to the middle of 1970 about 40,000 Swedish arrestees and 20,000 alien arrestees have been examined.

Figure 5 shows the percentage of male intravenous abusers in the Stockholm arrest population (Swedish citizens) arrested under the criminal code, and distributed according to age groups. The increase in prevalence is particularly marked among the youngest and the oldest age groups, where the rates increased tenfold from spring 1965 to spring 1967.

Figure 6 gives the percentage of abuse for Swedes arrested under the criminal code from spring 1965, and for men and women separately. The different drug policy periods have been marked. The prescribing of drugs to addicts for self-administration started on a rather small scale in 1965, and the rise in the prevalence was also moderate in that year. The prescribing increased rapidly during 1966 and culminated in the beginning of 1967. During this period the abuse rates increased rapidly from 24 percent to 38 percent of the total arrest population, but the increase in the absolute figures was even more marked (Table 3).

From the second half of 1967 there was a return to the traditional restrictive drug policy, and the increase in abuse was less steep. When the nationwide police offensive against the illegal drug trade was commenced on January 1, 1969, the abuse rates began to level off, and during the first half of 1970 they started to fall. During 1970 the police pressure on the drug trade was greatly reduced as the resources were not available to continue at the same intensity. Since little had been done about the

---

Figure 6. Percentage of drug abusers of intravenous type among male and female Swedes (<45 years) arrested under the criminal code in Stockholm, April 1965 to June 1970, related to changes in drug policy. Ninety-five percent confidence intervals marked. Manual calculations of the second quarter 1971, when the police offensive is over, show a steep increase in the percentage of abusers.

thousands of drug dependent persons circulating in the metro-politan area, the drug trade had time to reorganize and adapt to the new situation.

The illicit drug trade follows the same principles as normal trade. Profits are weighed against risks. In this field profits are

TABLE III

SWEDISH CITIZENS ARRESTED UNDER THE CRIMINAL CODE SHOW-ING SIGNS OF INTRAVENOUS DRUG ABUSE APRIL 1965 TO JUNE 1970

*Men*   A. Total number of abusers (1965 and 1970 incomplete years)

| *Age* | <15 | 15-19 | 20-24 | 25-29 | 30-34 | 35-39 | 40-44 | *Total* |
|---|---|---|---|---|---|---|---|---|
| 1965 | 0 | 50 | 207 | 137 | 85 | 46 | 4 | 529 |
| 1966 | 0 | 131 | 296 | 236 | 142 | 113 | 36 | 954 |
| 1967 | 1 | 397 | 532 | 398 | 237 | 189 | 119 | 1873 |
| 1968 | 1 | 483 | 660 | 522 | 303 | 202 | 122 | 2293 |
| 1969 | 3 | 433 | 696 | 550 | 297 | 179 | 153 | 2311 |
| 1970 | 0 | 167 | 252 | 241 | 130 | 58 | 56 | 905 |

B. Percentage of abusers

| | | | | | | | | |
|---|---|---|---|---|---|---|---|---|
| 1965 | 0.0 | 6.8 | 28.3 | 33.0 | 25.0 | 15.8 | 4.4 | 20.3 |
| 1966 | 0.0 | 12.8 | 27.7 | 36.6 | 28.4 | 21.6 | 18.6 | 24.0 |
| 1967 | 2.6 | 28.3 | 40.6 | 49.4 | 39.7 | 33.3 | 22.6 | 35.7 |
| 1968 | 2.2 | 30.7 | 48.7 | 55.5 | 46.5 | 33.3 | 23.1 | 40.2 |
| 1969 | 4.0 | 28.5 | 49.3 | 54.1 | 47.4 | 36.5 | 31.4 | 40.4 |
| 1970 | 0.0 | 21.5 | 40.5 | 51.2 | 46.1 | 26.7 | 27.3 | 34.9 |

*Women* A. Total number of abusers (1965 and 1970 incomplete years)

| | | | | | | | | |
|---|---|---|---|---|---|---|---|---|
| 1965 | 0 | 54 | 94 | 31 | 19 | 12 | 2 | 212 |
| 1966 | 3 | 107 | 106 | 43 | 16 | 12 | 9 | 296 |
| 1967 | 6 | 215 | 151 | 56 | 19 | 24 | 17 | 488 |
| 1968 | 6 | 219 | 183 | 99 | 31 | 26 | 25 | 589 |
| 1969 | 12 | 284 | 183 | 140 | 31 | 44 | 24 | 718 |
| 1970 | 3 | 110 | 78 | 56 | 11 | 11 | 10 | 279 |

B. Percentage of abusers

| | | | | | | | | |
|---|---|---|---|---|---|---|---|---|
| 1965 | 0.0 | 29.7 | 63.5 | 48.4 | 51.4 | 52.2 | 18.2 | 44.5 |
| 1966 | 7.7 | 34.1 | 63.1 | 58.9 | 42.1 | 25.0 | 52.9 | 42.5 |
| 1967 | 13.6 | 52.8 | 67.4 | 58.9 | 50.0 | 46.2 | 39.5 | 54.0 |
| 1968 | 18.8 | 52.0 | 72.6 | 76.2 | 63.3 | 60.5 | 54.3 | 60.5 |
| 1969 | 21.8 | 63.1 | 71.2 | 74.5 | 53.4 | 65.7 | 54.5 | 64.2 |
| 1970 | 13.6 | 57.9 | 70.9 | 73.7 | 37.9 | 68.8 | 47.6 | 60.1 |

*Note:* From Stockholm Police District.

enormous and risks moderate. For this reason there is no shortage of recruits from the underworld to fill the ranks depleted by arrests. As long as there is a large population of drug-hungry addicts, profits remain high and the effect of police hauls is to force up the price of drugs to maintain these profits. It seems to be impossible to check a drug epidemic without drastically reducing the demand for drugs, and this can only be done by removing a large proportion of the addicts from the drug market. It is worth noting that the Swedish police, during their offensive in 1969, were more effective than the Japanese police during their attack on the drug trade in 1954. The Swedish police arrested 14 percent of the estimated addict population for drug offenses, the Japanese police only 9 percent. In Japan, however, all drug offenders were taken out of the epidemic dynamics for a while. Swedish drug offenders could usually leave the arrest premises after interrogation, and were generally punished by fines, suspended sentences, psychiatric treatment, etc. Thus the basic conditions for the spread of addiction remained, and the epidemic has begun to increase again. While previously abuse was almost confined to central stimulants, there is now a widespread abuse of opiates also. There is some heroin, but the majority of opiate abusers are using morphine base smuggled into Sweden from middle and southern Europe.

## Chapter 7

# HOW CAN WE EXPLAIN MASS ADDICTION?

MANY PEOPLE consider that the main cause of the rapid spread of drug abuse is that society has become so uninteresting and life so lacking in meaning that the youth for this reason turn to drugs. This is a completely unsatisfactory explanation.

Is there anyone who is prepared to state that the social situation in Japan deteriorated so much from the end of the war to 1954 that it can explain the development of mass addiction during this period? And was the social situation so radically improved between 1955 and 1958?

What is the reason that the number of heroinists in England has doubled every sixteenth month during a decade, while in the U. S. the figures fell to a third in the 50 years following the introduction of the Harrison Act in 1914, while the population of the United States more than doubled during this period? And what has caused the steep increase in heroinism in the U. S. during the latter half of the sixties?

What is it that has gone wrong in Sweden since the beginning of the fifties, and which our Scandinavian neighbors have avoided until the middle of the sixties?

If we were to try to overcome the mass addiction of the type now raging in Sweden by first bringing forth a hardier population or by creating a society that is basically different, this would indeed lead us into a fatal and paralysing capitulation policy.

Only a clear understanding of the compulsive character of addiction, of the epidemic dynamic of mass abuse, and of the profit mechanism which steers the drug market can lead to effective countermeasures in the sphere of treatment and prevention.

## ADDICTED PHYSICIANS

The medical profession has an extremely high rate of addiction. About one percent of American doctors are said to be severely addicted. European investigations suggest that the problem is of the same proportion here. This makes addiction 30 to 50 times as frequent among physicians as among the general population in countries without a severe addiction epidemic. According to the argument that addiction is a symptom of psychological and social maladjustment, this should mean that maladjustment is 30 to 50 times as common among physicians as in the rest of the population!

What can we learn from addiction rates among physicians? What kind of doctors are affected, and how do they get on? We can establish the following:

1. *The ease with which the drugs are obtainable and their addicting propensity are the basic elements in development of addiction.* Doctors and nurses handle narcotic drugs daily, and can easily be tempted to administer them to themselves.

2. *Information and education seem to be very poor protection if the drugs are easily available.* Thus, not even a medical training provides adequate protection against addiction.

3. *No negative personality traits are required for the development of addiction if the drug is easily available.* The addict doctors in an American investigation did not prove to be deviating personalities, but were quite average people. It was noticed, however, that many of them had had unrealistic expectations of life and their future career. When they did not get as far as they had hoped, they became disappointed when they were 40 to 50 years of age and took to drugs, often in connection with pain or depression (Modlin and Montes, 1964).

4. *Extremely favorable social conditions do not protect people from addiction if the drugs are easily available.*

5. *A high socio-economic status is not in itself of any great significance in protecting against addiction.*

In the popular debate, abuse of drugs is not differentiated from addiction. There is a tendency to underestimate the force and character of the established drug dependence, which has a depth and power of basic drives, and may even be much stronger than sexual drives. At the same time it is common to overestimate the significance of various social supportive arrangements for persons already severely addicted.

Most of our intravenous addicts have many social difficulties to battle against: poor occupational training, with the result that they are referred to poorly paid work, and unemployment always affects them first; their economy is shaky even without addiction: many have housing difficulties; they have perhaps been thrown out of their homes, or they are divorced: many have a criminal past long before they began to abuse drugs.

For social and humanitarian reasons these people should receive support and help in every way. We shall, however, not expect this support to affect their addiction, any more than we would expect sexual desires to disappear under improved social conditions.

The addicted physicians had everything that our average addicts lack and can hardly hope to obtain: good occupational training and a good economy; good housing, usually a stable family situation with wife and children; a good social position to return to; extensive knowledge of what addiction really implies.

How do these specially favored addicts get on then? The American investigator, Pescor, after experience of treating them in hospital with a high standard of psychotherapy and other treatment, summarizes resignedly: "Yes, despite all these advantages, he is little, if any, better prospect for cure than the ordinary addict." On the other hand, reports have been published from California showing good rehabilitation results with addicted physicians under long, close supervision (Jones and Thompson, 1958, Quinn, 1958).

## MORTALITY IN ADDICTION

Apart from the fact that addicts usually function very poorly as individuals in the family and in society, they have a very high frequency of sickness of various kinds, more or less secondary to their addiction. Addiction is also always associated with a high death rate. *Preliminary investigations regarding intravenous abuse of central stimulants show that Swedish addicts have 15 to 25 times as high death rates as contemporary age groups.*

Even the addicted doctors have a very high death rate. Heroinists with legal prescription seem to fare worst. Of 100 of these patients treated at Tooting Bec Hospital in London, 13 were dead one year after discharge. It may be added that 44 then continued to take heroin, nine had gone over to other opiates, 19 were admitted to hospital, were in prison, or had gone abroad. Only 15 had ceased to take drugs—for the time being, it must be added (Bewley 1968). Experience tells us that many of these will relapse later. Just as with cancer treatment it is only after a five-year observation period that one can make a reasonably safe prognosis in addiction.

## Chapter 8

# TREATMENT OF ADDICTION

THERE IS very extensive internationl psychiatric literature which stresses the need for long-term treatment in addiction.

In Sweden there are very few addicts who have received any treatment worthy of mentioning. A fairly large number have been admitted to psychiatric hospitals for some days up to a few months. Many have had several short treatment periods of this type. As a rule they have discharged themselves or absconded during leave of absence or when they were allowed out in the hospital grounds.

The Swedish Drug Dependence Committee reported that *every addict admitted to hospital in Sweden for addiction had been hospitalized an average of five times during the year investigated.*

Short treatment periods give the patient, his relatives, the social organs, and in some cases even physicians the misleading idea that the individual has received proper treatment. After repeated relapses he is regarded as a chronic and incurable case.

## HOW SHOULD TREATMENT BE ORGANIZED?

Most physicians engaged in treatment of addicts agree that we need a number of small, closed psychiatric wards for the initial phase of treatment (in some cases detoxication, treatment of restlessness, various investigations and examinations, diagnosis etc.), and an increasing number consider addicts should be obliged to undergo treatment.

Following the initial phase, at least six months treatment is required which can either continue at the psychiatric hospital, if certain special arrangements are made, or it can be carried out in half open forms at a reliable distance from the old addiction milieux.

64

## Special Treatment of Opiate Addiction

On account of the severe abstinence symptoms in opiate addiction, detoxication is brought about by gradually lessening doses during a period of one or two weeks, and is then practically without distress to the patient. The American link organization Synanon, however, like the Negro organization the Black Muslims only accepts abrupt discontinuation of drugs without lessening doses like a kind of "purifying fire."

After the physical detoxication the craving for the drug remains for a very long time, and generally this leads to frequent relapses.

There is today, in theory, a very effective method of treatment for opiate addiction. This is the *methadone blockade method* which was introduced by the Americans Dole and Nyswander. The treatment is commenced during a few weeks in hospital with complete detoxication. This is followed by a period with increasing doses of the long acting morphine substitute, methadone, usually mixed in fruit juice. The doses are increased so slowly that no euphoria is experienced. When the body is "saturated" the morphinist-heroinist can no longer get a kick from his old drug, on condition that he continues to take a glass of methadone juice once a day at the treatment center or chemist shop. Methadone treatment is effective in theory, but in practice difficulties arise just because most morphinists-heroinists, in spite of all the problems involved, prefer to continue as addicts. Experienced field workers find that since no pressure is put upon addicts to remain in a methadone scheme once they have started, they tend to enter when there is a shortage of drugs on the market, and leave when the supply is plentiful again (Harney 1965). Methadone treatment schemes aiming at maintenance without saturation can only make matters worse by giving the addict a basic "legal" supply of opiates to supplement his illicit purchase, as well as tiding him over periods of shortage. No methadone treatment can prevent addicts from abusing other drugs, as central stimulants and barbiturates while in the methadone program. In Sweden in 1970 about 400 morphinists were known to the authorities and they have all been offered methadone blockade treatment, but only a small part have been willing to try the treatment and of these only a couple of dozen have managed to continue for any length of time.

The situation is reminiscent of the alcoholics' resistance to regular treatment with drugs of Antabuse® type (disulfiram). Despite the serious condition and all the complications, they are not prepared to deprive themselves of the effects of alcohol. (Antabuse is a drug which causes the patient to feel very ill if he drinks any alcohol.)

## Treatment in Private Homes

One arrangement that has been tried in Sweden is to board out young addicts in the families of farmers living in the thinly populated areas of northern Sweden. Social workers supervise these patients and the foster homes through frequent contact. The results have been rather good, and best of all for the youth who have settled down in the agricultural area instead of returning to the city. This form of treatment is extremely cheap compared to traditional institutional care. It is difficult, however, to find suitable foster homes, and this form of treatment is only rarely suitable for addicts over 20. For them we must find new treatment methods which are both practical and economically feasible.

## Therapeutic Villages

I have proposed that a series of small, therapeutic villages should be set up out in the countryside. After the initial hospital admission patients could be offered the opportunity of spending the rest of the treatment period in a village of this type.

Naturally the patients must be differentiated so that cases with a favorable prognosis would not be mixed with those who are intent on continuing their abuse at the earliest possible opportunity. Otherwise, men and women should be mixed and the patients should live as natural an everyday life as possible.

Activity should be centered around some little workshop, school, or training college and be led by qualified staff.

Patients who prefer traditional treatment in hospital should be allowed to stay there. Also, those who are so disturbed and destructive that the treatment staff and patient collective cannot manage them should be returned to mental hospitals.

Finally, it must not be forgotten that many addicts of epidemic type had severe personality disturbances long before they became addicted. A very large number of them have such deviating personalities that they would have been "doomed" to life-long maladjustment even if they had not become addicted.

We must therefore have realistic expectations and not believe that addiction treatment and rehabilitation, however good, will succeed in "curing" all addicts and returning them to a "normal" life.

## Aftercare

We know that long-term, active aftercare in the form of social support and occupational advice (psychotherapy, group activity, help with housing, work, economy, education etc.) is a very important complement to the institutional treatment period.

Aftercare must also involve a certain amount of "pressure" on the individual to readjust himself. Experience shows that the result will be far better with compulsory aftercare and parole.

Without a job and somewhere to live the patient has little chance of managing when he leaves the treatment scheme and relapses quickly. The long, expensive treatment has then only served as a temporary intermission in the development of his addiction. The question of aftercare homes of boardinghouse type is therefore essential. Even these can fail unless the home is led by competent staff with a real insight into the problem.

Voluntary staff members can be of great assistance in aftercare by undertaking probationary duties or by building small contact groups to support the ex-addicts who for the rest of their lives bear within them a latent drug dependence. Relapses of various degrees of severity are a constant threat, and they usually occur when the patient meets his old addict friends. The ex-addict should therefore be drawn into new groups and different environments.

## COMPULSORY VERSUS VOLUNTARY TREATMENT

In the debate on treatment of addiction the main issue of contention is between voluntary and compulsory treatment. Those advocating voluntary treatment declare that nothing can be achieved by force. Clinical experience has shown, however, that compulsory treatment, in the form of parole, gives better results than voluntary treatment (Valliant 1969, Kurland *et al.* 1969) although more cures would be expected from voluntary treatment programs, since, presumbly, a favorable selection of patients seeks treatment voluntarily. The need for coercion is largely due just to the fact that addiction is a condition with the character of a basic drive; the free will is put out of action in this sector of the personality. In practice we have to choose between the compulsive force of the destructive addiction and the force of compulsion to undergo treatment.

Among the best treatment results reported are those from Shek Kwu Chau Island in Hong Kong. Officially the patients seek treatment voluntarily, but usually under strong pressure from relatives or authorities, and they have to sign a contract binding them to remain on the treatment island six months and under a control program for three years. Another argument against voluntary treatment as the sole treatment principle is that most addicts avoid treatment if they know it will mean giving up drugs.

Most leading psychiatrists in the field of addiction now regard addiction as a contagious condition. Among those holding this view are, in America, Brill (Vice Chairman, New York State Narcotic Addiction Control Commission); Cameron (Chief, Drug Dependence Division of Pharmacology and Toxicology, WHO); and Jaffe (Director of Special Action Office for Drug Abuse Prevention, White House, Washington, D. C.); in England, de Alarcón; James; and Birdwood; in Scandinavia, Strömgren, author of the principle Scandinavian textbook on psychiatry; Alström; and Retterstøl. At the Scandinavian Congress of Psychiatry in 1969 and the World Congress of Psychiatry in 1971 this aspect of the problem was stressed in many papers, and I do not know of a single psychiatrist at these congresses who opposed the theory that addiction is a communicable condition.

It is generally accepted that in serious, contagious conditions the first duty of society is to protect susceptible individuals from exposure to infection. In conditions where treatment results are poor, as in addiction, prevention is all the more important. With a view to this we accept compulsory treatment of venereal diseases, although these are fairly easily cured, and in many contagious diseases we accept compulsory isolation of patients during treatment. Widespread epidemics of infectious diseases in the past were brought under control only when their contagious mode of spread was understood, and measures were taken to interrupt the dynamics of the epidemics. I believe that we will be able to control addiction epidemics also when we are prepared to draw the logical consequences of the contagious character of drug-taking behavior, and apply the following generally accepted epidemiological methods:

1. *To get rid of the actual agent where possible, that is, to eliminate the dangerous drugs from the social milieu.* This is a task for the customs and the police in the case of illegal manufacture, smuggling, and peddling.

It must be remembered that property crimes follow the same basic principles as other economic activity, and the enormous profits to be made in the drug trade are bound to draw organized criminality to this sector. It is essential to reduce the demand on the drug market by removing a considerable portion of the addict population and bringing them into a long-term treatment program. Under all circumstances, an ultra-permissive society has no chance of combatting the lucrative drug market.

It is up to the health authorities and the medical profession to see that there is more restrictive prescribing of addicting drugs than is the case at present.

2. *"Vaccination" of the population at risk.* This would take the form of information to the threatened groups of youth and others. In the same way, the whole society must be "indoctrinated" against addiction. If these forms of abuse are socially accepted or tolerated it is inevitable that new and larger groups will be drawn in. Tec (1971) stresses the importance of improved relations between parents and children as a form of immunization against drug abuse.

3. *Treating the addicts.* The addicts have the right to adequate treatment, but society on the other hand must have the right to demand that the patients cooperate in treatment.

4. *Long-term treatment of highly contagious cases.* What are we to do with those who cannot be cured and who are unable to manage any kind of satisfactory outpatient treatment, but continue in illicit drug affairs and in addition *continue to draw others into addiction?* The following are logical alternatives available to society: a) to hold these highly contagious chronics responsible according to drug legislation, and let the penal services take care of them; b) to treat them in closed wards in mental hospitals; c) to sanction them to handle drugs on their own, that is, to dismiss all indictments against them, or prescribe drugs for them, and be content to note, where possible, how many new victims they draw into their addiction; d) to ignore the problem and pretend it does not exist.

The last alternative is the easiest and the one which is usually followed in most countries.

I personally have proposed that we shall accept them just as chronic addicts, and allow them to receive their drugs under supervision of medical staff in an area remote from the large cities. There they could live in peace with their addiction in a community with their loved ones. These patients must, of course, receive sick pensions, and the relatives should be eligible to remunerative service for taking care of them.

These addicts would be free to leave their "drug community" if they wished; but then they must also conform to the ordinary laws of society with regard to drugs.

## THE ROLE OF PUBLIC OPINION

The most important measure in the present situation is to spread such comprehensive information on the serious character of addiction and its rapid spread in many industrial countries that a broad and strong public opinion demands that society mobilizes its resources and meets the threat with effective countermeasures—legislation, prevention, and adequate treatment.

In 1968 I visited Japan to study their successful methods of dealing with the postwar wave of addiction. I met several of the people who had organized the great counterattack on the amphetamine epidemic in the fifties. They explained that they had long known exactly how the problem should be met, but it was not until public opinion demanded that the mass abuse of drugs should be stopped that the authorities were able to take the far-reaching measures that were required. Only then was one of the worst drug epidemics in history eliminated in a few years.

# REFERENCES

de Alarcón, R.: The spread of heroin abuse in a community. *Bull Narcotics,* *21*:17-22 (No. 3), 1969.

Alström, C. H.: Society's struggle against contagious addictions. V World Congress of Psychiatry. Plenary Session. Mexico City 1971.

Bejerot, N.: Aktuell toxikomaniproblematik. *Läkartidningen, 62*:4231-4238 (No. 50), 1965.

—*Addiction and Society.* Springfield, Thomas, 1970.

—An epidemic of intravenous drug abuse studied in arrestees in Stockholm 1965-70 and compared to changes in drug policy. V World Congress of Psychiatry. Abstracts. La Prensa Médica Mexicana, Mexico City 1971.

Benaim, S., Horder, J. P. and Anderson, J.: The falling girls. Observations on the dynamics of a hysterical epidemic. V World Congress of Psychiatry Abstracts. La Prensa Médica Mexicana, Mexico City 1971.

Bewley, T., Ben-Arie, O. and James, I. P.: Morbidity and mortality from heroin dependence. 1. Survey of heroin addicts known to Home Office. *Brit Med J,* 725-729, 1968.

Bewley, T. and Ben-Arie, O.: Morbidity and mortality from heroin dependence. 2. Study of 100 consecutive inpatients. *Brit Med J,* 727-730, 1968.

Birdwood, G.: *The Willing Victim: A Parent's guide to Drug Abuse.* Secker & Warburg, London, 1969.

Brain Report. Drug addiction. The second report of the interdepartmental committee. Her Majesty's Stationery Office, London, 1965.

Brill, H.: Medical and delinquent addicts or drug abusers: A medical distinction of legal significance. *Hastings Law Journal, 19*:783-801 (No. 3), 1968.

Campbell, A. M. G., Evans, M., Thomson, J. L. G. and Williams, M. J.: Cerebral atrophy in young cannabis smokers. *Lancet, 2*:1219-1225 (No. 7736), 1971.

Chapple, P. A. and Marks, V.: Letter to the editor: The addiction epidemic. *Lancet, 1*:288-289, 1965.

Dole, V. P. and Nyswander, M. A.: A medical treatment for diacetylmorphine (heroin) addiction. A clinical trial with methadone hydrochloride. *JAMA, 193*:80-84 (No. 8), 1965.

Edery, H.: Cannabis—Pharmacology. International Symposium on Drug Addiction. Jerusalem 1970.

Glatt, M. M.: Reflections on heroin and cocaine addiction. *Lancet, 2*:171-172, 1965.

Harney, M. L.: Current trends in treatment of opiate addiction. International Narcotic Enforcement Officers Association 6th Annual Conference Report, 66-69, 1965.

Hölldobler, B.: Communication between ants and their guests. *Sci Am,* *224*:86-93 (No. 3), 1971.

James, I. P.: Correspondence. *Lancet, 1*:288, 1965.

Jones, L. E. and Thompson, W.: How 92% Beat the Dope Habit. Bulletin, Los Angeles County Medical Association, April 3, 1958.

Jonsson, G. and Kälvesten, A. L.: 222 Stockholmspojkar. Stockholms kommunalförvaltning, Stockholm 1964.

Lewin, L.: *Phantastica, Narcotic and Stimulating Drugs. Their Use and Abuse.* London, Routledge & Kegan Paul, 1964.

Modlin, H. C. and Montes, A.: Narcotics addiction in physicians. *Amer J Psychiat, 121*:358-365, 1964.

Moran, E.: Gambling as a form of dependence. *Br J Addict, 64*:419-428 (No. 3/4), 1970.

Olds, J. and Milner, P.: Positive reinforcement produced by electrical stimulation of septal area and other regions of rat brain. *J Comp Physiol Psychol, 47*:419-427, 1954.

Pescor, M. J.: Physician drug addicts. *Dis Ner Syst, 3*:2-3, 1942.

Quinn, W. F.: Narcotic Addiction in Physicians. Bulletin, Los Angeles County Medical Association, April 3, 1958.

Rado, S.: Fighting narcotic bondage and other forms of narcotic disorders. *Comp Psych, 4*:160-167, 1963.

Retterstøl, N. and Sund, A.: Drug addiction and habituation. *Acta Psychiatr Scand, 40* (suppl 179), 1964.

Seevers, M. H.: Drugs, monkeys, and men. *Mich Q Rev, 8*: (No. 1), 1969.

Tec, L.: Immunization against drug abuse. V World Congress of Psychiatry. Abstracts. La Prensa Médica Mexicana, Mexico City 1971.

United Nations Survey Team. *Report on the Economic and Social Needs of the Opium-Producing Areas of Thailand.* Bangkok, Nai Chaleo Chuntarasup, Printer and Publisher, 1967.

Vaillant, G. E.: If the drug abuser is a danger to himself, who should intervene? In Wittenborn, Brill, Smith and Wittenborn (Eds.): *Drugs and Youth.* Springfield, Thomas, 1969.

Wikler, A.: *Opiate Addiction: Psychological and Neurophysiological Aspects in Relation to Clinical Problems.* Springfield, Thomas, 1953.

# INDEX

75